PROTECTING CHILD

Preventing Child De

Protecting Children and Young People series

Sharon Vincent, *Learning from Child Deaths and Serious Abuse in Scotland* (2010)

Anne Stafford, Sharon Vincent and Nigel Parton (eds) *Child Protection Reform across the United Kingdom* (2010)

Kate Alexander and Anne Stafford, *Children and Organised Sport* (2011)

Also of interest:
David H. Stone *Injury Prevention in Children: A Primer for Students and Practitioners* (2011

See www.dunedinacademicpress.co.uk for details of all our titles

PROTECTING CHILDREN AND YOUNG PEOPLE

SERIES EDITORS

ANNE STAFFORD

The University of Edinburgh / NSPCC Centre for UK-wide Learning in Child Protection

and **SHARON VINCENT**

Centre for Health and Social Care Improvement, University of Wolverhampton

Preventing Child Deaths: Learning from Review

Sharon Vincent

DUNEDIN

EDINBURGH ◆ LONDON

First published in 2013 by
Dunedin Academic Press Ltd

Head Office:
Hudson House, 8 Albany Street,
Edinburgh EH1 3QB

London Office:
The Towers, 54 Vartry Road,
London N15 6PU

ISBN: 978–1–78046–011–6
ISSN: 1756–0691

British Library Cataloguing in Publication data
A catalogue record for this book is available from the British Library

Typeset by Makar Publishing Production
Printed by CPI Group (UK) Ltd., Croydon, CR0 4Y

CONTENTS

ACKNOWLEDGEMENTS

I would like to thank the Leverhulme Trust for providing the funding for me to visit Australia, New Zealand, the United States and Canada. It was an honour to be able to visit these countries and learn about their child death review processes and hear about their efforts to prevent child deaths. Thanks also to the University of Edinburgh, my former employer, for allowing me to take a year out to visit these countries.

Enormous thanks to all the experts within the field, who are too numerous to name in person, who were willing to share their knowledge and devote their time to speak to me. Your input was much appreciated and without your involvement this book would not have been written. I would like to mention in particular Teri Covington, Leah Bromfield, Gythlian Loveday, Rob Ryan and Pam Swinfield. I greatly appreciated your help in identifying useful contacts, and facilitating access to professionals. Thank you for the hospitality you showed to me as a visitor in a strange country. My thanks also to Elly Robinson and colleagues at the Australian Institute of Family Studies, who provided me with a desk with a wonderful view and much needed company while I was in Melbourne.

Finally I would like to thank Kate Alexander and members of our Editorial Advisory Board for kindly reading and commenting on drafts.

LIST OF ABBREVIATIONS

ACC	Accident Compensation Corporation
ACPC	Area Child Protection Committee
BASINET	Baby Abstracting System and Information NETwork
BASPCAN	British Association for the Study and Prevention of Child Abuse and Neglect
BCCS	British Columbia Coroners Service
CA	Children's Administration
CAN	child abuse and neglect
CAPTA	Child Abuse Prevention and Treatment Act
CCOPMM	Consultative Council on Obstetric and Paediatric Mortality and Morbidity
CDC	Centers for Disease Control and Prevention
CDCR	Child Deaths and Critical Reports
CDCRC	Child Death Case Review Committee
CDNDSC	Child Death, Near Death and Still Birth Commission
CDOP	Child Death Overview Panel
CDPH	California Department of Public Health
CDR	child death review
CDRT	Child Death Review Team
CDRU	Child Death Review Unit
CDSIRC	Child Death and Serious Injury Review Committee
CEMACH	Confidential Enquiry into Maternal and Child Health
CFR	child fatality review
CMCH	Center for Maternal and Child Health
CPAC	Child Protection Accountability Commission
CPS	Child Protection Service
CRU	Case Review Unit
CSSIW	Care and Social Services Inspectorate Wales
CYMRC	Child and Youth Mortality Review Committee
DCSF	Department for Children Schools and Families

DHB	District Health Board
DHS	Department of Human Services
DOCS	Department of Community Services
FCANS	Fatal Child Abuse and Neglect Surveillance
FIMR	Fetal and Infant Mortality Review
FTE	full time equivalent
GCFRP	Georgian Child Fatality Review Panel
ICD	International Classification of Diseases
IRU	Inquiries and Review Unit
LSCB	Local Safeguarding Children's Board
MCFD	Ministry of Children and Family Development
MCH	Maternal and Child Health
MCHB	Maternal and Child Health Bureau
MoJ	Ministry of Justice
NCCDR	National Center for Child Death Review
NSW	New South Wales
NT	the Northern Territory
OECD	Organisation for Economic Co-operation and Development
Ofsted	Office for Standards in Education, Children's Services and Skills
ONS	Office of National Statistics
PRUDiC	Procedural Response to Unexpected Deaths in Childhood
QPR	question, persuade, refer
RCPATH	Royal College of Pathologists
RCPCH	Royal College of Paediatrics and Child Health
RRT	rapid response team
SA	South Australia
SCR	Serious Case Review
SID	sudden infant death
SUDI	sudden unexpected deaths in infants
SUID	sudden unexpected infant death
VCDRC	Victorian Child Death Review Committee
WA	Western Australia
WHO	World Health Organization

INTRODUCTION

CHILD DEATH REVIEW

The focus of this book is child death review (CDR) and how the learning from CDR can help us prevent child deaths. Children rarely die, but when they do it is extremely tragic and we have a responsibility to families and communities to find out why they died. CDR, or child fatality review (CFR) as it is sometimes called, enables us to do this.

Evidence suggests that significant proportions of child deaths may be preventable (Pearson, 2008). By examining the circumstances of individual cases where children have died we can define the issues, identify risk and protective factors and develop effective prevention initiatives to help us prevent other deaths in the future (Christian and Sege, 2010).

> Child death review is a multi-agency process that systematically collects data concerning the biological, behavioural, environmental, and social determinants of injury over the child's life course. Child death review is therefore capable of generating the broad spectrum of data required for an ecological understanding of preventable child mortality, which recognises individual, community, and societal factors that interact at different levels to influence child health and well-being (Desapriya *et al.*, 2011).

The aim of the CDR process is to create a shared understanding of the circumstances leading to a child's death (Johnston and Covington, 2011). Multi-disciplinary review teams request and review records from agencies that had contact with the child or their family; they may also seek information from family members or from the community in which the child lived. After reviewing all the information from multiple sources they come up with findings, make recommendations and develop actions to help prevent future deaths (Douglas and Cunningham, 2008; Durfee *et al.*, 2002).

The data that is generated through CDR can tell us more about the circumstances of individual deaths than other sources of information, such as data from death certificates (Hochstadt, 2006). As well as examining the death itself CDR teams can also view events that precede the death and events that follow the death. They are better placed to define the causal pathway, the chain of events that led to an individual death, because they can identify pre-existing vulnerabilities and circumstances, as well as fatal events. They can look at how the various factors interacted with lethal consequences and identify points at which the pathway could have been interrupted.

CDR teams originated in the United States (US) in the late 1970s and were initially established to investigate abuse and neglect-related deaths. The first team was developed in Los Angeles County, California in 1978 by Michael Durfee (Bunting and Reid, 2005; Axford and Bullock, 2005) in response to concerns about the under-reporting of child-abuse deaths because of misclassification on death certificates. Durfee argued that national and state mortality statistics, which relied on the International Classification of Diseases (ICD) coding system to define cause of death on death certificates, underestimated child fatalities attributable to homicide and unintentional death. He argued that a multi-disciplinary review process, which involved information sharing among social services, law enforcement, child welfare, public health and the coroner, would reduce the risk of child-abuse and neglect-related deaths being misclassified (Johnston and Covington, 2011).

CDR processes now exist in almost every US state, and similar systems have been introduced in many other countries, including the United Kingdom (UK), Canada, Australia, New Zealand and Ireland (Johnston and Covington, 2011). Over time the focus of CDR has expanded from investigation of abuse and neglect deaths towards a public health model of prevention of child fatality, which involves systematic review of all child deaths from all causes from birth to adolescence (Christian and Sege, 2010; Durfee *et al.*, , 2002; Webster *et al.*, , 2003; Schnitzer and Ewigman, 2005). CDR findings have motivated prevention activities in the areas of motor vehicle crashes, drownings, fires, sudden infant deaths (SIDs), homicides, suicides and natural deaths and have led to important legislative and policy developments to protect children. This book considers CDR processes in a number of different countries and examines how the findings from CDR have been used to develop prevention initiatives.

COMPARATIVE RESEARCH STUDY

The origins of the book lie in a research study I undertook between 2010 and 2012. I had spent a number of years examining child deaths and serious cases and considering CDR processes across the UK, which culminated in the publication in 2010 of a book in this series entitled *Learning from Child Deaths and Serious Abuse*. I knew there was a lot to be learned from investigation of CDR processes and prevention initiatives in other countries and therefore proposed to undertake an international study. Its aim was to pool knowledge about CDR in Australia, New Zealand, North America and the UK to further understanding of why children die; and to identify good practice to inform policy and practice around prevention. A Leverhulme Research Fellowship enabled me to visit Australia, New Zealand, the US and Canada to find out about their CDR processes and prevention initiatives. The study considered:

- how child deaths are reviewed;
- what data is collected on child deaths in the UK, Australia, New Zealand and North America;
- what the data tells us about the main risk factors;
- whether the different approaches to CDR in these countries are congruent with a public health approach;
- whether review has been effective in reducing child deaths.

A case study approach was adopted comprising analysis of documents such as international, national and local child homicide and fatality statistics and annual reports of CDR teams; semi-structured interviews with more than a hundred key informants including policymakers, members of CDR teams, academics and practitioners; and in the US and UK observation of CDR meetings where cases were reviewed. I was unable to attend review meetings in Australia and New Zealand, because they are closed to outsiders for reasons of confidentiality. Eighteen case studies were included in the study:

- New South Wales;
- Victoria;
- Western Australia;
- Queensland;
- South Australia;
- New Zealand;
- California;
- Maryland;
- Colorado;
- Wisconsin;
- District of Columbia;
- Washington;
- Delaware;
- Georgia;
- British Columbia;
- Ontario;
- England;
- Wales.

New Zealand, England and Wales are case studies in their own right, because they all have a national system of CDR. In contrast, as will be seen in the first two chapters of this book, national review systems do not exist in Australia, the US or Canada. There is considerable regional variation in CDR processes in these countries, and for this reason a case comprises a single state or province in these countries rather than a country. The cases were selected to represent the range of different CDR systems in these countries.

Quotes from key informants are used to illustrate themes throughout the book. They have not been attributed to individuals to protect the identity of people who participated in the study.

STRUCTURE OF THE BOOK

The first four chapters are concerned with describing the various processes of CDR across and within countries. Chapter 1 outlines the national CDR process in New Zealand. It also provides an overview of CDR processes in Australia, focusing in particular on processes in New South Wales, Victoria, Queensland, South Australia and Western Australia. Chapter 2 examines CDR in the United States, focusing particularly on Maryland, California, Colorado, Georgia, the District of Columbia, Delaware, Washington and Wisconsin. It also outlines processes in Canada, specifically those in British Columbia and Ontario. Chapter 3 discusses the national CDR processes that have recently been introduced in England and Wales.

Following consideration of CDR processes in these countries, states and provinces, Chapter 4 offers a comparison of CDR processes across Australia, New Zealand, the US, Canada and the UK, identifying similarities and differences in relation to legislation, focus of review, funding, family involvement and data collection. Chapter 5 highlights key themes across countries in relation to types of death and risk factors. It also identifies some of the prevention initiatives that have been implemented at local, state and national level. Finally Chapter 6 considers issues surrounding the effectiveness and impact of CDR and looks at how the learning from CDR can be used to inform policy and practice and prevent child deaths.

TABLE OF STATUTES

CHAPTER 1

Child death review in New Zealand and Australia

Introduction

This chapter provides an overview of CDR processes in New Zealand and Australia. It begins by outlining the key characteristics of the national co-ordinated system in New Zealand. In contrast, because there are no federal requirements to undertake CDR in Australia there is no national system there and processes vary considerably across states and territories. The chapter outlines processes in New South Wales, Victoria, Queensland, Western Australia and South Australia.

NEW ZEALAND

In contrast to Australia where CDR is fragmented across different states and territories New Zealand has a national, co-ordinated system of review. 'It is now true to say New Zealand has a child and youth mortality review system that reaches every corner of the country' (CYMRC, 2009, p. iii).

New Zealand's model of local review, which is organised at health board level, drew heavily on the system of local reviews in the US, which is described in the next chapter. The substantial role of the Ministry of Health in terms of developing, implementing and financing CDR in New Zealand has ensured, however, that their system is far more centrally co-ordinated than that in the US.

In 2001 a Child and Youth Mortality Review Committee (CYMRC) was established by the Minister of Health under the provisions of the New Zealand Public Health and Disability Act 2000. The CYMRC is required to review and report to the Minister of Health on the deaths of all children and youth in New Zealand (aged twenty-eight days

Table 1.1 Overview of CDR processes in New Zealand and Australia

State/Country	Key players	Legislation	Scope of review
New Zealand	Local Child and Youth Mortality Review Groups located in District Health Boards; and a national Child and Youth Mortality Review Committee (CYMRC)	New Zealand Public Health and Disability Act 2000	All deaths aged 28 days to 25 years
New South Wales	NSW ombudsman's office; Child Death Review Team (CDRT) in the Children's Commissioner's office	Community Service Act 1993	All deaths 0–18 years
Victoria	The Consultative Council on Obstetric and Paediatric Mortality and Morbidity (CCOPMM); Office of Child Safety Commissioner Inquiries and Review Unit (IRU); Victorian Child Death Review Committee (VCDRC)	Public Health and Well Being Act 2008; Child Wellbeing and Safety Act 2005; The Child Protection Legislation Amendment Act 2009	CCOPMM review all deaths 0–18 years; IRU review cases known to the Department of Human Services
Queensland	Commission for Children and Young People and Guardian; Department of Communities Case Review Unit (CRU); Child Death Case Review Committee (CDCRC)	Child Protection Act 1999; Child Guardian Act 2000	The commission keeps a register of all deaths 0–18 years but do not review all cases; CRU review cases known to the Department of Communities
South Australia	Child Death and Serious Injury Review Committee (CDSIRC)	Children's Protection Act 1993; Children's Protection (Keeping Them Safe) Amendment Act 2005	All deaths 0–18 years
Western Australia	Ombudsman WA; Child Death Review Advisory Panel	Parliamentary Commissioner Amendment Act 2009	Cases known to the child protection system

up to twenty-five years) with a view to reducing these deaths and to continuous quality improvements through the promotion of ongoing quality assurance programmes. The decision to review cases up to twenty-five years was taken in line with World Health Organization (WHO) definitions. The CYMRC is also required to advise on any other matter related to mortality review that the minister specifies in writing and to develop strategic plans and methodologies that are designed to reduce morbidity and mortality and are relevant to the committee's functions. A new amendment to the Act recently moved the CDR function out of the Ministry of Health and into a new Health, Quality and Safety Commission.

To meet the requirements of the legislation the CYMRC developed a system of Local Child and Youth Mortality Review Groups in New Zealand's twenty District Health Boards (DHBs). The local groups collect detailed information on all child and youth deaths and enter this into a database held at the University of Otago to support national work on the context, circumstances or categories of deaths. Local groups are multi-disciplinary and include Maori representation. Coroners are not involved.

> 'Coroners have been quite clear that they do not want to be involved because they don't want to be biased and there's no chance for the parents to be represented in the system so they see that as a matter of justice, and being independent, that they have got to not participate, whereas if you go to America they are a core part of the review system. There are pluses and minuses. The pluses are that it feels quite a clean process, there's no prosecution, there's no issues about telling the coroner something that he might then do something about because our legislation stops us giving out identifiable information.'

Although coroners are not represented on local teams, at national level the chair of the national committee and the chief coroner have an ongoing, reasonably close relationship, and at the local level it is expected that there will be some connection so CDR groups and coroners give the same messages to the public.

The local groups provide a forum for agents from key organisations involved locally to meet together, share information and initiate changes that need to occur at a local or national level to prevent future deaths. They use the information gathered from review of deaths to define local and national issues and where appropriate develop recommendations that have the potential to reduce deaths in the future. Some local groups have subgroups and can combine deaths; others have insufficient numbers of deaths to do this.

> 'Our philosophy was we'll only change things if we have local involvement and local change and to get local change you need to have local ownership of the problem and so that's why there was a big push on local committees and getting the right people on the committee.'

The Department of Health provides funding to DHBs to review deaths using a per-capita formula based on the number of deaths. A 0.27 full time equivalent (FTE) co-ordinator is provided per ten deaths, costing a total of 1.5 million New Zealand dollars. The co-ordinators complete the database, talk to a range of agencies and gather local information about cases, including information from the media. They put together a genogram and timeline of the child's life and present cases at a monthly meeting. Local co-ordinators hold a teleconference every two weeks to discuss themes and share good practice, and there is a co-ordinators' and chairs' meeting once a year. Co-ordinators report that they find these meetings really useful.

> 'For example when I started there seemed to be a high number of young men hanging themselves and I couldn't get this into perspective without knowing what was happening all over New Zealand and it turned out that wasn't such an issue for other groups.'

The teleconferences also provide an opportunity for local co-ordinators to discuss new issues that are emerging: for example, they considered a new phenomenon they were witnessing known as the 'choking game', in which young people accidentally asphyxiate themselves playing a game. A local area may experience only one such death, and it is, therefore, useful for co-ordinators to be able to discuss issues with other co-ordinators who may have witnessed similar cases in other areas, to find out what they have done to tackle this.

New Zealand wanted to introduce a system of local review so they could bring people together who could talk about local systems and make local recommendations to bring about local change. However, a key strength of the New Zealand system is that they also have a national committee.

'Local review is useful because it brings together people who can talk about local systems. You get the right information because you have the right people and then you can make national recommendations and respond to themes that emerge.'

All local areas use the same recording template and enter data in the same way, so the national committee can use local data to make national recommendations in relation to themes that are identified as being national priorities.

New Zealand's data system

New Zealand spent many years constructing an excellent data system to support its CDR process. This national data collection system includes standardised information from review of individual deaths in district health board regions as well as national review of collated information. A single, centralised, secure-access database of all child deaths and deaths of young people up to and including age twenty-four has been in place since 2002. The database was based on the US national case reporting system, which is discussed in the next chapter, but in contrast to what has happened in the US central government in New Zealand supported the CDR process from the beginning and the Ministry of Health provided dedicated resources to every local team to ensure local co-ordinators entered data into a centralised database in the same way. A handbook provides basic guidance. People who are involved in CDR in New Zealand admit that local groups may do things a little differently, but the system is essentially as co-ordinated as it is probably possible to be.

The database is held at the University of Otago, where the New Zealand Mortality Review Data Group is contracted to manage mortality review data. Having university involvement is another advantage of the New Zealand system. Some organisations provide data directly to the database when a child dies. This data is automatically transferred and is held centrally by the data group. Local groups are automatically notified of this information when a child dies. After an individual death is reviewed local co-ordinators input additional local information to the database. The Mortality Review Data Group collates and analyses information held in the database for the national review group. The national group receive de-identified data from the data group. They review collated case information as well as locally identified issues and recommendations and provide a detailed overview of regional and national trends, which can then be used to inform prevention strategies and support recommendations at local and national level.

The data held on the database comes from nine different sources:

- births, deaths and marriages (Department of Internal Affairs);

- Ministry of Health;
- Child, Youth and Family (Ministry of Social Development);
- Water Safety New Zealand;
- coroners;
- coronial services (Ministry of Justice);
- Ministry of Transport;
- Local Child and Youth Mortality Review Groups;
- families of the deceased.

The data group cleans the data. It enters and codes all information from the disparate and sometimes conflicting data sources to help facilitate local review as well as national reporting. Individuals involved in CDR in New Zealand acknowledge that building a good database can be very time-consuming. They have put a lot of time and effort into improving their data. It took them three years to decide what data to collect and only after five years did they concede that they had enough cases to undertake meaningful analysis at a national level. The research capacity is, however, now enormous. The database includes detailed quantitative and qualitative data. People involved in CDR in New Zealand believe that the quality of their quantitative analysis is good, but they acknowledge that they have as yet failed to utilise all the possibilities that the qualitative data offers. 'One day we might be able to start comparing the data across countries and this would expand the research potential further.'

In comparison with many other countries the CDR system in New Zealand is well co-ordinated and fits neatly together, but some local groups report that they would like more information from the national group.

> 'It can feel a little bit like the local groups are reviewing a large number of cases, but if there's no feedback from the national group then you're not getting a sense of the overall trends. Because they're looking at the aggregated data, which we don't see, sometimes it's been a little bit frustrating because we don't have a sense of what's being looked at nationally ... There's a lot of flow up because all our data is going into a national database but the flow back hasn't been quite ... they are trying to improve it but that's probably one of the weaknesses from a local level. We get the national report that's released once a year but that's really the only formal form of communication from the national committee.'

Ten members appointed by the Minister for Health are represented on the national group, plus a number of advisers. The national group makes recommendations to the Minister of Health, to professionals and to members of the public.

The legislation underpinning the CDR system in New Zealand is strong, and agencies can be fined for non-compliance if they fail to provide information. Local groups can obtain information from everyone except police and coroners, who can share information if they choose to do so.

There has only been limited involvement of families in New Zealand. There is a form on the website that families can use but in practice they rarely do.

> 'Our system doesn't have any feedback to parents. Parents can have access to the national report and they can go to the public website and input information but there's no feedback to them … It hasn't been very successful in having parents' input. If a parent goes online and inputs information it's not unreasonable to think they might have some information come back to them. It would be quite a hard situation for a parent in that situation to get their head round. But that sometimes is a gap in our reviews because we sometimes still have lots of questions and we just can't answer them because we can't understand what the dynamic in the family was or what might have precipitated a certain event.'

Local teams reported that they used to be able to see transcripts of interviews that the police had done with families, which enabled them to obtain additional information about the families, but they are no longer able to access this information.

In addition to the local and national CDR process the Office of the Chief Social Worker can review deaths in New Zealand in cases where the child is, or was, known to their department in the twelve months prior to their death. This process is not rooted in legislation. The Office of the Chief Social Worker continues to review some cases, but the majority of deaths of children known to the department are now reviewed through local CDR review.

> 'At one time they would have reviewed all deaths known to the department ... They've stepped back since December 08 and they only now review deaths from homicide or suicide or where circumstances surrounding the death warrant further inquiry ... so they've really narrowed ... We're grappling with what is child and youth mortality's role going to be in looking at those cases given that they have an expectation now that we're doing the full review.'

The Office of the Chief Social Worker makes a decision about whether or not to include families in the review process on a case-by-case basis.

> 'In one case that I was working on we interviewed the maternal grandmother, and we interviewed an aunty and uncle who were also the caregivers of the surviving children and got a lot of really great information from that and what we've found is that families are really quite pleased to talk to us. It's relatively new that we actually talk to family. Before it used to be very much organisational — we'd talk to staff, we'd do the case review based on the files but we shied away from the family. I think my feeling is we weren't quite sure how to approach them and there is that kind of — you know — sensitivity about that. But what we've realised now is they hold a really important key into how we might be able to improve practice in the future. So what we do generally is we get in touch with them first off and tell them that we're doing this review and we want to see if there are things we could've done differently. We try to approach it as sensitively as possible and give them a chance to say if they don't want to talk to us. They don't have to and that's fine, and what we've found is that families want to talk to us and also families tend to be interested in us improving our practice as well so they see it as a really useful tool for us to do things a bit better. So we approach them, we usually set up a time, we'll go to them, so that means we'll go all around the country side to do what we need to do to get their views. Usually there are two of us that go, so we'll have

someone asking the questions and leading that part and someone who's taking the notes. We give them the chance if they want to bring support people. So we just leave the ball in their court, we just ask questions about 'tell us about your involvement with the child; what are the things that you see as strengths with what child youth and family did; and do you think we could have done things a bit differently but better?' and try to get the key, from their point of view, the key points in this child's life where things could have taken a different pathway, you know sort of a particular stage where things might have been different. So that's just useful because oftentimes I think we go around thinking one thing and they see things in a whole other point of view and it's a real, I think our team thinks it's a privilege that we get a chance to talk to the family and sometimes we're doing it not long after this child has died as well and you know they're still grieving and it's still a really awful time for them. And so the idea is that once we've written up our report that we'll go back to them and we tell them that we'll come back to them. We'll travel to where they are and we'll give them a chance to read the section of the report that we think is the bit that they've contributed to. Whether or not they read the whole report that's something that we determine as and when what might be appropriate. So we don't have really any hard and fast rules about what we do — we kind of just go with the flow of the family.'

The Children's Commissioner's Office also has the power to investigate child deaths in New Zealand but has undertaken only two such investigations.

AUSTRALIA

Of the eight states and territories in Australia New South Wales (NSW), the Northern Territory (NT), Queensland, South Australia (SA), Victoria and Western Australia (WA) have some sort of CDR team or committee (Lamont, 2010). The Northern Territory Care and Protection of Children Act 2007 included provisions for the establishment of a Child Death Review and Prevention Committee, which is required to establish and maintain a child death register for all child deaths in the NT (and children whose usual residence is in the NT) up to the age of eighteen years (Lamont, 2010). The Child Death Review and Prevention Committee has to keep a register of the deaths of all children up to eighteen but does not have to review all cases. As yet Tasmania and the Australian Capital Territory have no legislative or operational frameworks in place to enable the review and reporting of child deaths (Newton *et al.*, 2010). The Child Death and Serious Injury Council of Tasmania Bill will, however, amend the Children, Young Persons and their Families Act 1997 to introduce processes in Tasmania.

CDR processes vary considerably across Australia. Those states and territories that have a CDR system only review cases at state/territory level; in contrast to New Zealand there are no local review systems in Australia. The different systems are underpinned by very different legislative and operational frameworks, and they vary considerably in terms of level of independence and scope of review (Newton *et al.*, 2010). In some states deaths of children known to the child protection system are prioritised.

> A number of Australian jurisdictions focus primarily on practice in the statutory child protection service, and deal with the wider service system only incidentally. It can be argued that this is a missed opportunity in terms of systemic learning, and may contribute to child protection workers feeling blamed and that they are carrying the responsibility for an entire service system. A more useful approach would be a broad multi-sectoral inquiry that involves all the agencies and systems associated with the child and family (Gibbs, 2009, p. 13).

Some states have one system of review for all deaths and a separate review system for deaths of children known to the child protection system.

It is common in Australia for states to have a two-tier system of CDR whereby one body undertakes reviews and another provides an oversight role, but some states or territories have a single-tier review system. The considerable variability across states and territories means it is not possible to obtain reliable national data about child deaths in Australia: 'It is lamentable that these inconsistencies have resulted in an inability to establish reliable Australian national data about child protection deaths for comparison and research' (Gibbs, 2009, p. 2).

Newton *et al.* (2010) overviewed the different systems of CDR across Australia, focusing particularly on New South Wales, Victoria and Queensland, and concluded that the complexities were contributing to Australia's failure to prevent the deaths of children within the child protection system. They argued for more comparability between states and offered a framework of key items that should be present in CDR legislation to make for better comprehension and more comparability between states.

New South Wales

A number of different organisations are involved in CDR in NSW.

> 'In NSW it's a bit of a complex system because there's a lot of us engaged in CDR but from slightly different angles'.

NSW has had a system of CDR since 1996, when the Child Protection Council made a recommendation for a CDR team following the review of a number of child deaths. The Office for Children and Young People set up a children's commissioner, and CDR was brought under the responsibility of the commissioner. Over time the focus of review changed from deaths from assault to epidemiological review.

> 'Deaths from abuse were rare, it was less about reviewing them and more about preventing them. Reviewing those deaths was a fruitless exercise ... We got to the point where we had a good CDR system ... we could substantially influence child well-being through the use of death data. The child well-being framework made it work. CDR was located in an agency that could bring together research, policy, communication and awareness and legislation,'

The Department of Community Services (DOCS) set up its own internal review process to review deaths known to the department in 2004. The Child Deaths and Critical Reports (CDCR) unit review process placed an emphasis on learning and developing a feedback loop back into policy and practice.

The NSW government chose to reform the CDR system in 2008, following recommendations made in the Wood inquiry. This was a special commission of inquiry into child protection services in NSW, which responded to the high-profile deaths of two children — Dean Shillingsworth and Ebony (Wood, 2008). The two children were from different families but died in close proximity to each other in 2007; both had had extensive involvement with DOCS, NSW's child protection service, prior to their deaths. The role of CDR came under considerable scrutiny in the Wood inquiry. It identified duplication of work by different bodies and made recommendations for a clearer delineation of roles in relation to CDR and a more streamlined process for each agency.

Following the Wood inquiry, since November 2009 the ombudsman is now the convenor of the CDRT and the Commissioner for Children and Young People is now a member of the team.

> 'One of the reasons the reviewable death function moved to the ombudsman is because of the power of inquiry that the ombudsman had.'

The CDR team is a multi-disciplinary one that was and remains responsible for reviewing the deaths of all children in NSW from birth to seventeen. They have a strong research function and undertake specialised research to prevent or reduce child deaths. The ombudsman reviews deaths:

- that may have been due to abuse or neglect;
- that occurred in suspicious circumstances;
- where a child is in care or a detention centre;
- where a child is in disability services.

The ombudsman has royal commission powers and can secure records from any agency, including private ones.

Prior to 2009 the ombudsman and the DOCS CDCR unit were both involved in reviewing the deaths of children known to DOCS. Since 2009 the ombudsman no longer has this function. CDCR reviews the deaths of all children known to DOCS within three years of their death, regardless of how they died. Reviewers undertake initial reviews on all deaths known to DOCS and more comprehensive reviews of some deaths to identify systemic and practice issues for organisational learning and improvement. On occasion they may also examine critical incidents. Initial reviews include information from the coroner, a summary of DOCS involvement with the family, and analysis of casework based on review of electronic case records and policy, procedures and guidelines. Comprehensive reviews include analysis of casework file information, interviews with DOCS staff and analysis of relevant literature and research. The special commission of inquiry recommended that CDCR continues to review cases known to DOCS. It concluded that CDCR's organisational learning focus was a unique and effective strategy to influence casework practice, especially the practice reviews it undertakes, which provide staff with the opportunity to reflect on practice and discuss ideas for practice improvement drawing on research, data from CDCR and practice methods. (These are discussed in Chapter 6.)

Victoria

The Consultative Council on Obstetric and Paediatric Mortality and Morbidity (CCOPMM), a statutory body established under the Public Health and Well Being Act 2008, advises the Minister for Health on mortality, perinatal and paediatric deaths. It has a public health surveillance, reporting and research role in relation to all deaths of children aged 0–18 that occur in Victoria. When a child dies the medical practitioner who certifies the death prepares a report for the CCOPMM, which includes a range of demographic and descriptive data. The CCOPMM reviews and reports on all deaths. The 2008 legislation enables it to request information from anybody who provided care to the child, including, for example, professionals in a childcare facility or a teacher. In practice, however, members of the CCOPMM report that it can be difficult to obtain the names of people involved with the child if they are located outside of health. Many of its recommendations are, therefore, directed towards health agencies, although they do have a public health focus and also look at systems issues and have covered issues such as transfer between states, pool fencing and farm safety.

Victoria has a two-tiered review system for examining case practice and service provision in cases where children who have died were clients of the Department of Human Services (DHS) Child Protection Service (CPS) at the time of, or within twelve months of, their death. The death of each child is examined individually, and then in aggregate, to identify common themes and emerging trends. The Child Well Being and Safety Act 2005 contained provisions regarding the conduct of child death inquiries. The Act states that the aim of such inquiries is to 'promote continuous improvement and innovation in policies and practices relating to child protection and safety' (Section 33(2)).

The Office of the Child Safety Commissioner Inquiries and Review Unit (IRU) undertakes inquiries in collaboration with external case analysts, who are appointed to provide expert advice. They review the services provided, or omitted to be provided, to the client. A reflective practice approach is used, and the aim of the process is to distil learning and to influence future policy and practice. The Child Protection Legislation Amendment Act 2009 amended the provisions of the Child Well Being and Safety Act 2005. The 2009 Act increased the number of cases that IRU reviews by extending the length of contact with the CPS from three months prior to the child's death to twelve months. It also enabled the IRU to review serious incident cases as well as deaths. In theory Section 19 of the legislation permits the Minister for Community Services to ask the IRU to review cases that are not known to the child protection system, but in practice this has not happened to date.

IRU's methodology includes review of DHS child protection electronic and paper files, and of other agencies' files where appropriate, and interviewing of DHS child protection staff and other professionals involved with the child and family. Parents and other primary caregivers are also contacted and participate in around half of cases.

> 'We are the only ones who talk to parents. It's a way of remembering a child's life. Parents appreciate the opportunity to be heard, they don't always feel they are heard by child protection. It gives them a chance to salvage something from the tragedy.'

A section in each review report is devoted to the parents' perspective. Parents have not participated in any abuse and neglect cases, but these constitute a very small proportion of cases.

Although staff from other agencies can be interviewed they do not have to participate. Inquiry reports are sent to the Victorian Child Death Review Committee (VCDRC), which constitutes the second tier of review. The VCDRC is an independent, multi-disciplinary ministerial advisory board comprising a chair and eleven other members. It looks at every case and makes recommendations in relation to that case; it also makes recommendations in relation to clusters of cases. The key contribution of VCDRC is to identify common themes and emerging trends across cases that have been subject to child death inquiries to inform ongoing system reform.

> While each individual child death inquiry identifies factors unique to each child's death, the review function of the VCDRC ensures that collective learning across cases is identified and used to inform ongoing system reform across all levels of programme, policy and practice development (VCDRC, 2008, p. 31).

The VCDRC provides an annual report to the Minister of Community Services, which is tabled in parliament as part of the commitment in Victoria to a transparent and accountable response to deaths of children within the child protection population.

South Australia

The Child Death and Serious Injury Review Committee (CDSIRC) reviews the circumstances and causes of death and serious injuries to children in SA from birth to eighteen years. It is a statutory body with powers of review across all government departments into all causes of child deaths and serious injuries. The CDSIRC was established in February 2006 by Part 7C of the Children's Protection Act 1993, and its role is to contribute to the prevention of death or serious injury to children in SA. It arose out of recommendations made by the Layton review of child protection services in 2003 (Layton, 2003).

The CDSIRC identifies changes in legislation, policy, practice or procedure and makes recommendations to government that may help prevent similar deaths or serious injuries. The Children's Protection

(Keeping Them Safe) Amendment Act 2005 authorises the CDSIRC to:

- maintain a database of the circumstances and causes of child death or serious injury that occur in SA;
- review child deaths and serious injury with the aim of identifying legislative or administrative means of preventing similar deaths or injuries;
- request any person to produce a document that is relevant to a review;
- enter into arrangements with other government agencies for the release of information relevant to a review;
- recommend legislative or administrative change based on its reviews;
- monitor the implementation of its recommendations;
- maintain links with similar bodies interstate and overseas.

The powers and functions of the CDSIRC are unique compared to other states: the committee has the dual functions of keeping a database of the circumstances and causes of child deaths and of conducting in-depth reviews. In other jurisdictions these functions are the responsibility of different agencies.

The CDSIRC is not required to review all cases of death or serious injury, and is prevented by legislation from undertaking a review unless there is no risk it would compromise an ongoing criminal investigation or coronial inquiry. However, it has information on all deaths, and its focus is not just deaths of children known to the child protection system but also any child who may have died from actual or suspected abuse or neglect, children in detention, children under the care and protection of the minister and cases referred by the coroner. The CDSIRC also considers deaths where the circumstances suggest systematic changes could be made to prevent similar deaths or serious injuries: for example, deaths associated with product or environmental safety. The fact that the CDSIRC also has legislative responsibility for review of serious injury is another factor that sets it apart from its counterparts in most other states in Australia.

> Opportunities for prevention can be identified through the systematic collection and analysis of morbidity and

> mortality data and through the analysis of the circumstances surrounding particular child deaths and serious injuries. Improvements to child-focused systems and services, and changes to legislation, policies or practices can assist in the prevention of further deaths and injuries, and contribute to reducing human and financial costs to the community (CDSIRC, 2010, p. 31).

The CDSIRC is limited to the review of relevant reports and records and does not interview staff — unlike many other jurisdictions in Australia. Unlike many other states, too, it has the legislative power to obtain information from many different sources, including the coroner, courts and non-government organisations as well as health and education ones. Reviews are submitted to the Minister for Families and Communities for consideration and implementation of any recommendations, and the CDSIRC has a statutory obligation to monitor implementation of its recommendations. The minister seeks responses from relevant portfolios and service providers and collates and returns responses to the CDSIRC, which is funded through the Keeping Them Safe initiative, with further contributions from the Department for Families and Communities, Department of Health and Department of Education and Children's Services.

The CDSIRC is divided into different teams that consider different types of death. There are those for medical deaths, fatal assault or neglect deaths, suicides, drownings and transport-based deaths.

> 'It means each team develops its own expertise.'

These groups meet three or four times a month and decide which cases should be subject to in-depth review.

The Adverse Events review process is a separate internal review mechanism within Families South Australia (the state child welfare authority) for reviewing the deaths and serious injuries of children known to, or whose families were known to, Families South Australia. Reviewers examine all case documentation and relevant legislation, policy and procedural documentation. They are also able to interview staff, but staff are not compelled to participate.

Queensland

> 'The quality of reviews has increased, they are now more focused on learning, the aim is to improve practice and prevent deaths but the main way to prevent deaths is to improve practice.'

Queensland has a two-tier system for reviewing the deaths of children known to the child protection system in the three years before their death. The first tier of review is undertaken by the Department of Communities regarding its involvement with the child in accordance with Section 246A of the Child Protection Act 1999. The department's CRU, part of Complaints and Review, which sits within the Office of the Director General, facilitates and conducts reviews, although in some circumstances an external reviewer may be appointed to undertake a case if, for example, there is a lot of media attention surrounding the case or if the child is in care.

The CRU may undertake a limited or a detailed review. Limited reviews are undertaken if the threshold for a detailed review is not met. They involve analysis of file material and discussion with only the relevant manager or regional director. Detailed reviews are undertaken where there are issues that impacted on the department's service delivery to the child. These include discussions with staff involved in service delivery as well as review of file materials. The aim of a detailed review is to understand the reasons for the decision-making that occurred. The internal Systems and Practice Review Committee considers the review report and its recommendations.

The report and all materials used to inform the review are then passed to the external Child Death Case Review Committee (CDCRC), which comprises the second tier of review. This is an independent, multi-disciplinary mandated body made up of the Commissioner for Children and Young People and Child Guardian as chair, the assistant commissioner and up to seven other members who are appointed by the minister. In accordance with Chapter 6 of the Commission for Children and Young People and Child Guardian Act 2000, the CDCRC must assess the department's review against a set of review criteria and provide a report back to the department; it can also make its own recommendations for improving service delivery. The

CRU can write to and talk to staff in any department but it can only review the practice of, and make recommendations to, child safety. The CDCRC is also only able to make recommendations to child safety. This is recognised as a significant challenge. CDCRC would like formal powers to be able to refer to other agencies and has considered changing the legislation in Queensland to enable this.

The Commission for Children and Young People also maintains a child death register of all child deaths, which is compiled using information from births, deaths and marriages and the police. It publishes two annual reports: one from the case review committee on deaths of children known to the department; the other of all deaths of children aged 0–17 years in Queensland, which is more of a statistical report. It does not review individual cases for all deaths but looks at single issues across a range of cases such as suicide.

Western Australia

The process of CDR was recently reformed in WA. As in NSW in June 2009, the ombudsman WA took over responsibility for reviewing and investigating child deaths following the passage of the Parliamentary Commissioner Amendment Act 2009. Child death reviews were previously performed by the Western Australian CDR Committee (Lamont, 2010), a ministerially appointed committee supported by parliament, which was set up following a recommendation in the Gordon inquiry — an aboriginal specific inquiry.

> 'The main, and I think only, disadvantage of the old system was that it only looked at the Department of Child Protection. It had no power really to do anything outside of that department whereas the ombudsman's office has authority to review all departments. They're not restricted to only a single department and that was the major issue.'

In contrast the ombudsman's office has much stronger powers. It can interview staff from any agency and make recommendations to any agency, whereas prior to reform recommendations could only be made to the Department of Child Protection.

> 'We're able to in terms of our investigative powers interview anyone we need to interview. We have royal commission

> powers. If we need to, even staff from the non-government sector can be required to talk to us about what they do and their role in the life of the child.'

Not all deaths are reviewed in WA. Specific categories of deaths are reviewed in a single-tier system of review.

> 'We're interested in preventable deaths and quite reasonably we don't want to direct resources to, or put the department through, an investigation unless it's really going to be for some kind of learning that's going to prevent deaths in the future. So that's our focus — it's about preventable deaths and what can we learn from the death of a child that's just occurred.'

The Department for Child Protection receives information from the state coroner on all sudden or unexpected deaths including those from non-natural causes or where the cause is not known. The department notifies the ombudsman of these deaths and of children who have died in its care. It provides the ombudsman with a copy of the coroner's notification and a summary of any involvement of the department with the child, or a child relative of the child; it also offers a view as to whether the death is an investigable death.

The ombudsman examines all child death notifications received and determines whether the death is investigable as defined by Section 19 A (3) of the Parliamentary Commissioner Act 1971. Investigable deaths are defined as having some involvement with the child protection system, but include cases where there was a single report of concern regarding the child's well-being, which resulted in no action being taken. If a case does not meet the criteria a report is completed and any issues noted. If it is considered investigable a review is conducted, either a simple review where there are no administrative issues relating to the department or any other public authority, or a more detailed one where files and contacts are requested. In addition to reviewing the circumstances in which individual children died and looking at why they died, the ombudsman's function is also to identify any patterns or trends in relation to deaths, and to make recommendations to any department or authority about ways to prevent or reduce investigable deaths.

Although WA has a single tier of review the ombudsman has set up a Child Death Review Advisory Panel to provide independent advice. The panel meets four times a year and comprises six members with a range of expertise.

CONCLUSION

- New Zealand has a mandated, nationally co-ordinated, government-funded local CDR process that reviews all deaths of all children.
- There are no federal requirements to undertake CDR in Australia, so there is no national co-ordination and considerable variation exists across states and territories. Review is mandated and funded, but is undertaken at state not local level, and the focus of review varies across states from all deaths to deaths of children known only to child protection agencies.
- All local teams in New Zealand input data into a national database, which now has extensive, good-quality national data on the deaths of all children and young people up to twenty-five years; reliable national data is not available in Australia.
- With the exception of Victoria, Australian states have not tended to involve families in the review process; families can be involved in New Zealand but rarely are.

CHAPTER 2

Child Death Review in North America

Introduction

There are no federal requirements to undertake CDR in the US or in Canada, and this has led to considerable variability across states and provinces in both countries. This chapter begins by providing an overview of CDR processes in the US. It then considers processes in Maryland, California, Colorado, Georgia, the District of Columbia, Delaware, Washington and Wisconsin. These states comprise the full range of CDR models in operation in the US, including: state review only; state and local review; state and regional review; and local review only. They also comprise: states where CDR is funded and states where it is not; states where CDR is rooted in legislation and states where it is not; and states that use the national case recording tool and those that do not. The chapter then moves on to look at Canada, where child deaths are reviewed at only provincial level. In contrast to the US and New Zealand, but in comparison with Australia, reviews are not undertaken at local level in Canada. The chapter describes processes of review in British Columbia and Ontario.

UNITED STATES OF AMERICA

Despite the fact that the goals of the federal government's US Healthy People 2020 (US Department of Health and Human Services, 2010) include review by a CDR team of all deaths of children under eighteen because of external causes, there are actually no federal requirements to undertake CDR in the US and no federal funding is provided for this. In contrast, federal funding is provided for Fetal and Infant Mortality Review (FIMR) — a separate but related review process. States can and do, however, use federal grants such as the maternal

Table 2.1 Overview of CDR processes in the US and Canada

State/ province	Key players	Legislation	Scope of review
Maryland	State and local Child Fatality Review Team in the Center for Maternal and Child Health	Mandated under the Maryland Senate Bill 464	All causes of deaths 0–18 years received by the Office of the Chief Medical Examiner
California	Local CDRTs; California Department of Public Health (CDPH) Fatal Child Abuse and Neglect Surveillance (FCANS) programme	Local teams are permitted but not mandated under the Penal Code; there is a mandate to track data on fatal child abuse and neglect	There is a mandate to review abuse and neglect deaths, but most teams review all sudden, traumatic and/or unexpected child deaths (i.e. coroner cases) up to 18 years
Colorado	State and local Child Fatality Prevention Review team in the Department of Public Health and Environment	Mandated under the Colorado House Bill 05–1280	Legislation specifies review of deaths of children 0–18 years receiving services from a county department of social services, or where there has been a report of suspected abuse or neglect; however, all unexpected and unexplained deaths of children 0–18 years are reviewed
Georgia	Georgian Child Fatality Review Panel (GCFRP) and local review teams in the Office of the Child Advocate	Mandated under Section 19–15–1 *et seq.*	All injury, SIDs, unexpected or unattended physical deaths to children up to 18 years
District of Columbia	State Child Fatality Review Committee in the Office of the Chief Medical Examiner	Mandated under mayor Executive Order (D.C. Act 14–40)	Deaths from all causes 0–18 years
Delaware	State Child Death, Near Death and Still Birth Commission (CDNDSC) in the Administrative Offices of the Court; and regional child death panels	Mandated under Delaware Code Title 31, Chapter 3	Deaths of children up to 18 years, near deaths of abused and/or neglected children and stillbirths occurring after at least 20 weeks of gestation
Washington	Local CDRTs; State Department of Health	Local teams are authorised not mandated under Statute 70.05.170; legislation requires the State Department of Health to assist with data entry and technical assistance and encourage communication among local teams	Each local review team is different; most review all unexpected deaths up to 18 years
Wisconsin	State and local CDRTs in the Children's Health Alliance	None	Varies but the state team recommends review up to and including 18 years
British Columbia	Child Death Review Unit British Columbia Coroners Service (BCCS)	Coroners Act (RSBC 2007)	All deaths 18 years and under from all causes
Ontario	Coroners Service — Under Five Child Death Committee and Paediatric Death Committee	Coroners Act 1990	All deaths under 5 years; all deaths known to a Children's Aid Society; medically complex deaths where there are concerns regarding medical care

and child health block grant to fund CDR. Lack of national leadership and co-ordination means there is wide variation in structures across the US (Webster *et al.*, 2003). CDR processes are different in each state and trying to establish any kind of national picture in the US is, therefore, very complex, although generally the US tends to favour local review, as in New Zealand and England. Iowa is the only US state that does not have a CDR system. Some states have state and local review teams and have a local team in every county. This means there are a large number of local teams in some states: for example, 159 in Georgia. Other states, for example, Delaware, have regional teams that cover several counties. The advantage of regional teams is most obvious in rural areas, where child fatalities are rare, as is the expertise needed to staff the team (Hochstadt, 2006). In states that have state and local review processes the state team does not always review cases. Instead its role may be to support local teams and make state-level recommendations based on analysis of aggregate data. A small number of states, for example, the District of Columbia, have state review only, and their model of CDR is more akin to that in some Australian states and Canadian provinces.

CDR in the US

- Thirty-one states undertake state level review;
- Thirty-five states undertake county level review;
- Seventeen states undertake state and county review;
- One state does not review child deaths at state or county level (NCCDR, 2011).

Legislation

- Thirty-seven states have mandated state CDR;
- Seven states have no legislation for state CDR;
- In seven states legislation permits but does not mandate state CDR;
- Fifteen states have mandatory local CDR;
- Eighteen states have no legislation for local CDR;
- Eighteen states have legislation permitting but not mandating local CDR (Covington, 2011).

Over time CDR in the US has moved from being located in child welfare or justice to being placed in public health (as it was from the outset in New Zealand). However, social services still co-ordinate CDR in eleven states including Illinois and New York; and in a small number of states the function is located in the medical examiner's or coroner's office (as it is in Canada) or within justice (Covington, 2011; NCCDR, 2011).

The focus of review has expanded over time in line with change in location. Many CDR teams initially reviewed only abuse and neglect cases, but in the mid to late 1990s the US Maternal and Child Health Bureau and other national organisations demanded a broader focus for CDR and expansion of review to all potentially preventable deaths (Johnston and Covington, 2011). Most teams now, therefore, review all deaths up to age eighteen and some review deaths up to twenty-five years, as in New Zealand. Some states, for example, California, have a mandate to review abuse and neglect deaths only, but they often choose to review other deaths as well.

As in Australia, New Zealand and the UK most US states have maintained separate internal agency review processes for reviewing deaths of children known to CPSs. In some states, however, for example Delaware, review of abuse and neglect cases has been integrated within the overall model of CDR, although review may be undertaken by a separate review team. As in SA eleven US states undertake serious injury reviews in addition to child death reviews.

The funding situation for CDR in the US is generally unstable. The median income of CDR teams is falling, and some states have no funding at all (Covington, 2011). Where funding is provided it is more likely to be through federal funds, but some states do use general state funds.

The considerable variation in structures of CDR across states means there is no standardised method of data collection, making comparability of child death data between states and the identification of national trends virtually impossible (Bunting and Reid, 2005). However, thirty-six US states use a standardised, web-based case reporting system developed by the National Center for Child Death Review (NCCDR). The NCCDR is custodian of a national database that contains extensive information on more than 88,000 child deaths across the US. The system was designed to inform improvements in child safety and prevent deaths, and NCCDR uses the data to inform federal agencies and influence national policy.

The US National Center for Child Death Review

The US Government Maternal and Child Health Bureau (MCHB) provides some funding for a national resource centre – the US NCCDR. NCCDR's website (at www.childdeathreview.org) includes state annual reports and other reports, best practice tools and state spotlights. The NCCDR was funded in 2002 to explore the feasibility of building a standardised reporting tool for local and state CDR teams. It found that forty-four of fifty states had some form of case reporting tool, but there was little consistency in the type of information that was being collected and analysed (Covington, 2011). A National Case Reporting System was developed to provide CDR teams with a method for capturing, analysing and reporting on the full set of information shared at a child death or serious injury review. States that use the system are able to download their data on an annual basis and can generate annual reports on all deaths reviewed as well as specialised reports on specific types of deaths such as suicides or drownings.

Despite its large size the US has made significant progress in sharing good practice across states. The MCHB fund an annual meeting of state co-ordinators, and the federally funded NCCDR has an extremely informative website, which includes best practice tools. Regional coalitions of states meet to share good practice, and site visits have taken place across teams with similar child-death profiles.

Most US states do not involve families in CDR.

> 'One of the things we miss here in the United States is the component of the family element which the UK has and British Columbia uses in their CDR. When we think about a child and learning what was going on in that child's life those days before they died who best knows that than family members or caregivers? And we don't offer that opportunity to families to give input like they're doing in the UK and what British Columbia's doing … those that do respond back it's a great empowerment opportunity to learn that their child didn't die in vain and that other people are trying to learn from that death. And I think that's our biggest weakness in the United States.'

Many people involved in CDR in the US are, however, of the opinion that it is inappropriate to involve families.

> 'Because the goal of the team is investigation and really to talk about how these disciplines all come together it's not in anyone's best interests and personally I don't even think it's in the family's best interests. There's a lot of things that maybe the family don't want to know that was going on.'

The absence of family involvement in the CDR process contrasts with the FIMR process in the US, where the maternal interview is a key component. A FIMR social worker attempts to reach each mother within fifteen months of the death of the child by sending two letters and making three phone attempts. If the social worker is able to make contact with the mother, she explains the purpose of the FIMR programme and requests a maternal interview. If the mother agrees to the interview, it is scheduled at a time and place of her convenience and comfort. The social worker provides written grief information that is specific to the mother's experience and makes any necessary referrals for counselling or support. Some states have attempted to evaluate the maternal interview process. For example, in Delaware women are sent an evaluation form to complete about their experience of the interview process to make sure they feel they are benefiting from participation and not being harmed. Based on nineteen evaluations returned, eighteen mothers felt the interview gave them an opportunity to share their feelings. Women reported that they chose to do the interviews in order: to provide information that might help other mothers and infants; to talk about their experience; and to obtain help finding services.

Maryland

Maryland has had mandatory state and local CDR teams since 1999. CDR is located in the Center for Maternal and Child Health (CMCH), in the Department of Health and Mental Hygiene along with the FIMR programme, but it is not funded. The state team is a multi-disciplinary team composed of at least twenty-five members appointed by the governor, including eleven people with expertise or interest in child safety or welfare, twelve representatives from state agencies and two paediatricians; there is also a full-time state co-ordinator. The team meets quarterly. The purpose of the state team is to:

- prevent child deaths by developing an understanding of the causes and incidence of child deaths;
- develop plans for implementing changes within the agencies represented on the state team to prevent child deaths;
- advise the governor, General Assembly, and the public on changes to law, policy and practice to prevent child death.

There are twenty-three local, county-based review teams and one city team. Local teams advocate at the local level through letters to the media and recommendations to agencies. They also identify education and training needs at the local level. The state team has created a policy manual of guidelines to assist local teams. Legislation requires that local teams review the deaths of children aged 0–18 years, but they can elect to review deaths up to 21 years. They review all causes of deaths that are notified to the Office of the Chief Medical Examiner, i.e. all unusual and unexpected deaths, and use the NCCDR case-reporting system to record information about these deaths.

The state team does not review cases. It uses data collected from vital statistics, injury prevention, highway safety and local reviews to make recommendations to the legislature and to community action groups aimed at preventing child deaths. It is required to submit an annual report to the governor and hold training and education events for local teams.

California

Prevention is the overriding priority of CDR in California, where CDR teams have several objectives. These are to:

- assist in identifying and investigating potential child maltreatment cases;
- assist in protecting siblings and other children;
- identify and assist in improving agency and systems problems;
- prevent future child deaths from all causes through identifying the circumstances surrounding child deaths and developing recommendations and effective action.

California currently only has local CDR; it does not have a state team. The legislation permits, but does not mandate, local and state review. A state CDR council was set up in 1982, but it is contingent on funds being available and was disbanded in 2008, when state funds were cut. Local teams have been functioning in California since the early 1980s, with Los Angeles County being the first place to establish a team in 1978. Most counties followed suit and continue to have CDR teams, despite the fact that they are only formally authorised, as opposed to mandated, in statute. Fifty to fifty-five local teams are active at any time. A network of regional CDR team co-ordinators used to meet quarterly to maintain communication among local teams and state agencies, but this was disbanded along with the state council. Under a new state statute, if county teams exist they are required to make their findings and aggregate data available annually, and many teams now produce annual reports that are available to the general public.

Legislation stipulates that teams should investigate deaths relating to abuse and neglect, but most teams choose to review all sudden, traumatic and/or unexpected child deaths (i.e., coroner cases), including injury, natural and undetermined deaths. Review selection criteria vary by team, but generally teams review all sudden and expected deaths of children under eighteen years old.

The Sacramento local team examines all deaths from all causes, and a Youth Death Subcommittee undertakes more in-depth reviews of all deaths of young people aged ten and over. There is also a Prevention Advisory Committee comprising a broader group of people than those that hold case-specific information and review cases. The Prevention Advisory Committee reviews aggregate data, determines what this means in terms of prevention and community risk factors and makes recommendations. It is currently producing a report based on twenty years of aggregated data.

Although the state CDR team has been disbanded the California Department of Public Health (CDPH) still has a mandate to track data on fatal child abuse and neglect, and in 2000 it created the Fatal Child Abuse and Neglect Surveillance (FCANS) programme to fulfil this obligation. Funds for the programme were cut in 2008, but 0.25 FTE staff time is provided by the Centers for Disease Control and

Prevention (CDC) block grant, and approximately $150,000 of local assistance money from the federal Maternal Child Health Grant is used to support local teams including training on data collection, writing effective recommendations and taking findings to action. Local teams use the NCCDR case-reporting system. They complete standardised data reporting forms for all mandated cases and for most other cases as well. The state FCANS programme aggregates the data from local teams and manages the state data, but an annual state report has not been produced for several years due to budget cuts.

California reconciliation audit for better identification of child-maltreatment-related deaths

The FCANS programme conducts a reconciliation audit to identify and accurately count child-maltreatment-related deaths. The audit is based on multiple state (i.e., vital statistics, supplemental homicide reports, child abuse central index, child welfare services/case management system) and local (i.e., CDR team) data sources, using CDR teams as the 'alloy' standard (i.e., not a gold standard, but the best standard available based on local CDR and multiple sources). Audit results confirm that the process of using CDR teams to reconcile multiple data sources identifies a significantly higher number of child-maltreatment-related deaths than any single state data source.

Colorado

Colorado has a state and local CDR system, which was established by legislative mandate in 2005. The new legislation replaced the Colorado Child Fatality Review Committee, which had been established in 1989 by an inter-agency agreement between the departments of Human Service and Public Health and Environment. CDR is located in the Department of Public Health and Environment and financed in part by Maternal and Child Health (MCH) block funds and Child Abuse Prevention and Treatment Act (CAPTA) federal funds. The legislation mandates a large state team of forty-five members, including seventeen governor appointments, sixteen state agency representatives, and twelve professionals selected by discipline. The state team meets quarterly to discuss case review findings, prevention recommendations and policy issues. Separate subcommittees discuss deaths from natural causes, unintentional injuries, violence-related deaths, motor vehicle crashes, child abuse and neglect deaths, and SIDs and undetermined deaths. One full-time member of staff co-ordinates the system and the state review team, serves on the state's Maternal Mortality Review Committee, and provides administration support. There are currently five local teams operating in Colorado. In contrast to some other states the state team does not provide oversight or funding to local teams, but some training has been given.

Cases where children were receiving services from a county department of social services, or in which there has been a report of suspected abuse or neglect, must be reviewed in Colorado, but the records of all other unexpected and unexplained deaths of children from birth to eighteen are also reviewed in order to develop a community approach to the prevention of child fatalities. The purpose of review is to understand the incidence and causes of childhood deaths and to identify any gaps in service delivery of public agencies serving children and families.

The NCCDR's standardised data reporting forms are completed for all reviews. State annual reports are not produced, but data reports and statistical briefs based on multiple years of findings and specific topic areas have been published when funding has been available. The state team is, however, mandated to report recommendations for changes to law, rule or policy that it determines will promote the safety and well-being of children in Colorado. It must also produce a report annually for the governor, the Senate and House Health and Human Services Committees and the Senate as well as the House Judiciary Committees of the Colorado General Assembly.

Georgia

The main purpose of Georgia's CDR programme is to prevent deaths and serve Georgia's children: by promoting more accurate identification and reporting of child fatalities; by evaluating the prevalence and circumstances of both child abuse cases and child fatality investigations; and by monitoring the implementation and impact of the statewide child injury prevention plan in order to prevent and reduce incidents of child abuse and fatalities in the state.

State and local review teams were established by statute in 1990. CDR is administered by the Office of the Child Advocate and funded through the Children's Justice Act, CDC Sudden Unexpected Infant Death (SUID — the American term for Sudden Unexpected Deaths in Infants/SUDI) grant and state general funds. An annual budget of $303,511 provides four full-time employees and one contract employee at state level. The state team comprises seventeen members, who meet quarterly to oversee the local CDR process, report to the governor annually on the incidence of child deaths and recommend prevention measures based on the data. The state team provides monthly training for local teams and coroners across the state, including a 'beginner's' introduction to CDR processes for newly elected coroners.

There are 159 local teams, each of which has seven mandated members who are directed to meet within thirty days of a child's death. A prevention advocate must be represented on each local team. Teams review all injury, SIDs, and unexpected or unattended physical deaths to children under eighteen years old. The NCCDR's standardised data reporting forms are completed for all reviews, and state vital statistics are used as a form of quality assurance to ensure that all appropriate deaths are captured for review. The Division of Public Health aggregates and analyses the data and distributes an annual report to the governor, lieutenant governor, Speaker of the House and members of the community.

District of Columbia

The District of Columbia has a state CDR system only, which was established by statute in 1992. In contrast to most other states review is not undertaken at local level. The CDR programme is located in the Office of the Chief Medical Examiner, which is fairly unusual in the US but more common in Canada. An annual budget of approximately $300,000 from District of Columbia appropriations pays for three full-time employees.

The purpose of the state committee is to prevent child deaths and to improve child, youth and family service delivery systems. It is required to produce an annual report, which is made available to the public and distributed to the mayor and committee members. The state committee consists of around thirty-five members appointed by the mayor, and it is required to have two chairs, one of which must be a paediatrician. Eight members of the public, recommended from each ward council, are represented on the committee. There are two case review teams — the Child Fatality Review team and the Infant Mortality Review team, which meet twice a month. The committee reviews deaths from all causes to children from birth to eighteen years and can choose to review cases beyond this (up to twenty-five years) if the child was known to Juvenile Justice, Child Welfare or the Mental Retardation and Developmental Disabilities Systems. Training is provided to all new review team members.

Standardised data reporting forms are completed for all reviews and required by policy, but the District of Columbia uses its own state system it does not use the NCCDR case reporting tool.

Delaware

Delaware has a state and regional CDR process that was established by legislation in 1995. The Child Death, Near Death and Still Birth Commission (CDNDSC), which can be compared to the state review teams found in other states, is located in the administrative offices of the Court. It is located there for administrative purposes only, not because Delaware has a justice model of CDR that can be contrasted with the public health model in many other states. A fiscal note was attached to the legislation in 2004 to provide funding for three dedicated staff positions from general state funds, to support the CDNDSC; in 2006, FIMR's budgetary positions were also placed within the commission.

The CDNDSC's mission is to safeguard the children of Delaware by examining the deaths of children under eighteen years old. Reviews are undertaken on the deaths of all children under eighteen, as well as near deaths of abused and/or neglected children and stillbirths occurring after at least twenty weeks of gestation.

The commission can establish up to three regional child death panels, which conduct monthly reviews, and it meets at least quarterly to review and approve the work of the panels as well as the FIMR case review teams. The Newcastle and Kent/Sussex Review Panel examines all non-child abuse or neglect deaths and the Child Abuse/Neglect Review Panel reviews deaths and near deaths due to child abuse and neglect across the state. Abuse and neglect cases go through an expedited review process: the CDNDSC is required to investigate and review all the facts and circumstances of the death or near death within three months of notification; there is then a final review process after criminal investigations are finalised.

This system was introduced in an attempt to alleviate any immediate system concerns that may have contributed to the death or near death. System-wide recommendations arising from an expedited review must go to the governor and General Assembly, as well as any members of the public requesting the recommendations, within twenty days of the completion of an investigation and review. A near death is defined as a child in serious or critical condition as a result of child abuse or neglect as determined by a physician. The chair of the Child Protection Accountability Commission (CPAC) is a member of the CDNDSC, and the legislation specifies that the two commissions must meet at least annually to discuss recommendations and system improvements.

Standardised data reporting forms are required by state policy and are completed for all reviews using the NCCDR case recording tool. The FIMR programme uses the database Baby Abstracting System and Information NETwork (BASINET), supported by Go Beyond, LLC , and data from both databases is used to complete an annual report, which includes trends and recommendations. Although it makes sense to complete one annual report based on combined data from CDR and FIMR this is unusual, and most states produce separate reports. Statute requires that the NCCDR produces an annual report, but this has not happened every year because of fiscal constraints. The report is distributed to public officials and interested citizens.

Washington

In 1993 local public health agencies in Washington were authorised by statute to conduct child death reviews, but they are not required to undertake them.

> 'You're allowed to but you're not required to and there's no money behind it.'

A few agencies began conducting reviews, but the CDR programme was not developed as a statewide system until 1997, when an annual budget of $500,000 was provided to the Washington State Department of Health from state general funds. Some $350,000 of the total budget was contracted out to local county health departments in the state to support the co-ordination of local review teams. The remaining $150,000 supported two full-time staff at state level to co-ordinate a data collection and analysis system, provide training and technical assistance to local teams, disseminate recommendations and other data reports, convene a State Advisory Committee and provide oversight of the statewide programme.

Unfortunately funding for this programme was withdrawn in 2003. Some local teams continue to operate, and the Department of Health continues to provide limited support. In 2009 legislation was passed requiring the Department of Health to assist local health departments with data entry, provide technical assistance and encourage communication among local teams, but the legislation specified that this be funded through federal and private funding only. Two state employees at 0.25 FTE each funded by the MCH block grant currently fulfil this obligation.

Until funding was lost in 2003 all counties reviewed all child deaths, there was a robust database of state information and a state panel.

> 'Now we're not capturing statewide all child fatality in any kind of a co-ordinated way ... as soon as that funding disappeared the whole system fell apart. There wasn't a lot of commitment locally to do this, to keep the process going.'

Seventeen out of thirty-five of the original local teams continue to operate on some level.

> 'We have to work out how to work in the most efficient way because there's no funding for this process.'

Most local teams review all unexpected deaths of children aged seventeen and under, excluding those due to extreme prematurity, but each local team is different: for example, in King County the co-ordinator chooses which cases to review each month and normally excludes natural deaths. The team tends to review groups of similar cases together, so they can invite experts. Local teams receive a list of deaths from the medical examiner's office, but medical examiners do not receive notification of all deaths: for example, cases where children have died in hospital of natural causes do not go to the medical examiner.

The NCCDR standardised data reporting forms are completed for all reviews, but data collection is not required by legislation or policy. Vital statistics are used to match death data with files in the CDR database to assure that all eligible deaths have been reviewed. Department of Health assessment staff administer the data system, analyse the data for CDR reports, and provide specialised data for reports and presentations on request, but a state annual report is no longer produced.

The Department of Health Office of Maternal and Child Health sponsored a CDR conference for CDR teams and partners in 2009 funded by a technical assistance grant from the federal MCHB.

There is a separate but parallel system of CDR in the Children's Administration for review of cases in which the agency has had involvement with the family in the last twelve months. These reviews are case specific, and a report is written on each case, which includes recommendations. Systemic issues can be noted, but the Children's Administration (CA) cannot tell other agencies what to do. The reports are redacted and placed on a public website. The CA does not have to wait for a criminal investigation to finish before undertaking these reviews. The ombudsman provides oversight by reviewing all of the reports and following up on recommendations. There is some overlap between these reviews and those undertaken by CDR, as all of the cases reviewed by the CA will also be subject to CDR.

> 'We did have one case that we shared and it was really useful to see how different the two processes are. The purpose of the King Country CDR is to drive prevention and we typically have four to seven cases in a two-hour time slot we're not looking at it in depth. The purpose of the CA's is to look at where the responsibility was and if they carried it out. It's a totally different process. The CA review is also a huge review of documents. It covers the entire span of the involvement of the family with the department so you really go all the way back. And some of their reviews we've been there all day'.

Under new legislation, cases will be reviewed only by the CA if there are suspicions of abuse and neglect; near fatalities will also be reviewed. The process will be more multi-disciplinary and include external members.

Wisconsin

Wisconsin has state and local CDR teams. The state programme was established in 1998 and was initially founded under the Children's Justice Act federal grant and situated in the Department of Justice, but it has been located within the Children's Health Alliance since 2005 with partial funding provided through the Department of Justice, the Children's Justice Act grant programme and the University of Wisconsin School of Medicine and Public Health Wisconsin Partnership Program.

> 'It was a natural transition for us given that we use the public health prevention model and a lot of our leadership comes from local health departments and because we would get all deaths — not just abuse and neglect ones — the state prosecutor's office didn't make a lot of sense ... the department is still a critical partner and they still provide some funding.'

A full-time staff member provides data and epidemiology support. Funding for this is given through a three-year grant from the University of Wisconsin School of Medicine and Public Health Wisconsin Partnership Program. The grant was awarded to the Children's Health Alliance, in partnership with the Injury Research Center at the Medical Center of Wisconsin.

> '... not only so local counties can get their data out of the case reporting system but even to put their data in. They really need a lot of help.'

Funding also provides 3.5 FTE staff at the state level. A new three-year grant has recently been awarded to build a FIMR system for Wisconsin that will collaborate with the CDR system.

CDR is not yet mandated in Wisconsin, but legislation is being drafted.

> 'It will make a difference having legislation, the local community struggle with confidentiality.'

Because CDR is not currently rooted in legislation people involved in review report that information sharing can be problematic. The new legislation will require all agencies to share information.

> 'There are a ridiculous amount of forms to fill in. Because we don't have legislation we've had to craft a confidentiality package. The first thing teams do is sign a memorandum of understanding with their local Vital Records. This allows them to get death certificates from their county and then they sign a memorandum of understanding with all of the core agencies.'

The state council does not review cases; it considers aggregate data and makes recommendations for legislative change. The state team comprises twenty-four members, who meet four times a year. It has four primary goals, to:

- advise the legislature and state agencies on the need for modifications to law, policy or practice;
- educate the public regarding the incidence and causes of child deaths, and specific steps the public can take to prevent future deaths;
- identify training needs and make training resources available to professional organisations, advocacy groups and others statewide;
- facilitate the development of local/regional CDR teams.

In 2008 there were ten local teams in Wisconsin; there are now thirty-six. The state team has produced a manual called *Keeping Kids Alive in Wisconsin: CDRT Guidelines* (Children's Health Alliance of Wisconsin, n.d.) to provide counties with step-by-step assistance on how to organise and implement a CDR team. It is based on the NCCDR model but is 'summarised down into a Wisconsin version. We took out things that didn't apply to us and we added things that do apply to us. Really in theory a team could take this guidebook and implement themselves ... it's very descriptive that's intentional.'

The state team also provides additional technical assistance related to data collection and prevention to teams. Annual statewide training is given, bringing together most local teams. This training focuses on improving the quality of reviews, sharing new information and networking. Regional and local trainings are also held annually.

> 'We expect them to catalyse prevention but we don't expect them to do the prevention. I don't know if that's unique to Wisconsin or not, but our CDR teams are not experts in prevention. We might have members that are like the Safekids coalition or the health department to some extent ... but we want them to transition this to groups in the community that are already doing this kind of prevention ... we want them to look at whose already doing it in their community ... we have some communities that stay more directly involved in prevention, and then we have other communities that are very hands off, and then some that are kind of in the middle.'

All local teams review all deaths of children up to and including eighteen years old, and some, particularly smaller teams, review deaths up to age twenty-five. In addition, some teams review all domestic violence deaths and all suicides regardless of age, so they include adult deaths as well. One local team also reviews injury cases, and it is written into the new legislation that teams can do this.

Wisconsin uses the NCCDR case reporting system, but local teams can choose whether or not they wish to enter data into the system and twenty-four of the thirty-six teams choose to do this. Of the eight local teams who do not enter data two have CDR processes but have not yet had any child deaths to review. A third of all child deaths in Wisconsin are now included in the data system.

CANADA

There are no federal requirements to undertake CDR in Canada. Each province is different. Most provinces have processes for reviewing deaths of children known to the child welfare system, but more comprehensive CDR processes only exist in a small number of provinces. In those provinces that have CDR this is undertaken at provincial not local level. CDR systems in Canada are, therefore, more akin to state-based processes in Australia than to the predominantly local-based systems of the US, New Zealand and England.

British Columbia

Between 1996 and 2002 CDRs in BC were undertaken by the Children's Commission, which was created following the Gove inquiry. The commission had a mandate to review all child deaths, so all deaths of young people under nineteen were reported to them, but the focus was on unexpected deaths and particularly on review of the deaths of children in care or known to the child welfare system. Following a review of government services the Children's Commission was disbanded and the function of CDR was transferred to the coroner's service and the advocacy role of the Children's Commission was transferred to a new advocate. With the move to the coroner the focus of CDR transferred from deaths of children in the child welfare service to all child deaths, but there was no legislation to support this change and the coroner's budget had been reduced.

> 'So it was really a lame duck between 2003 and 2007 and during those years there were a number of high-profile tragedies in the child welfare system. In 2005 the child welfare system here in BC was under investigation … The whole child welfare system came under horrendous scrutiny.'

Deaths of children in care were subject to a public inquiry in 2005 by Ted Hughes. The report of the review came out in 2006 and made a number of recommendations to strengthen the child welfare system, which included the creation of the Representative for Children and Youth and the endorsement that the CDR function stay within the coroner's service but be supported by a budget and legislation (Hughes, 2006).

CDR in BC is now undertaken by a team within the coroner's service, which is an agency within the Ministry of Public Safety and Solicitor General. Review is undertaken at provincial not local level. The BC Child Death Review Unit (CDRU) has a legislative mandate to review, on an aggregate or individual basis, the facts and circumstances of the deaths of all children aged eighteen and under. The unit's mandate is to understand better how and why children die, and to make recommendations for action to prevent future deaths and improve the health, safety and well-being of children in BC. Under Section 48 of the Coroners Act RSBC 2007, CDRU members are authorised to review coroner files, exercise powers of investigation, and seize additional information required to inform the review process (Desapriya *et al.*, 2011).

In comparison with other countries it is unusual for the CDR function to be located within the coroner's office, although as we have seen CDR is located within the medical examiner's office in the District of Columbia and new CDR processes in the Northern Territory in Australia are also placed within the coroner's office. People involved in CDR in BC concede that being located in the coroner's office can present challenges, not least because the coroner's focus is death investigations whereas CDR tends to fit more within a public health/epidemiology framework.

> 'There's a craft, there's a practice of CDR that's very different from doing question-and-answer and investigation ... and we've worked really hard at trying to embrace the CDR craft in the context of what could be seen as a very bad fit for us.'

However, the coroner in BC, in contrast to the coroner in other countries, has the power to investigate every child death — not just sudden or unexpected deaths — so the fit may make more sense than in other countries.

> 'We believe there are lessons to be learned from looking at the other deaths even though most of these deaths are probably not preventable ... Within that population of natural, expected deaths we were finding that a small number of those cases were not natural expected deaths.'

There is dedicated funding for CDR in BC, but the budget has been cut substantially in recent years. The CDRU consists of a director, programme assistant and case reviewers. Appointed under the Coroners Act 2007, reviewers have the authority to exercise powers of investigation, including the ability to obtain additional information when required to complete a case review. The methodology used by the

CRU is based on best practices for CDR from across North America.

The review process consists of three main components: case reviews; recommendation development, implementation and monitoring; and reporting on CDRU activities and review findings. Each case is assigned to a reviewer after the coroner has completed their investigation or when an inquest is complete. The reviewer conducts an initial examination of the coroner's file and gathers additional information from health, schools, police, the family and other agencies. They then complete a protocol that captures data on demographics, circumstances and risk factors relevant to the child's death. This data is entered into the coroner's service database and is used to look at patterns and trends. The reviewers also produce a case summary, which captures the child's story — what happened in the child's life and around the death. A definitions document has been developed, which usefully defines exactly what each term means. Cases are then presented at multi-disciplinary team meetings.

> 'This enables discussion. We go back and forth and we get to the kernel of the truth or as close to that as we can get through consensus.'

Depending on the nature of the case external experts may be brought in. As in England the team determines whether a death was preventable. In 2009 60% of 262 cases reviewed were determined to be preventable (CDRU, 2010).

> A preventable death is one in which, with retrospective analysis, it is determined that a reasonable prevention at the individual, community or system level may have prevented the death through modification of one or more risk factors (CDRU, 2010, p. 13).

Family involvement in British Columbia

Families are always involved in CDR in BC. The review team routinely sends a letter to the family to let them know they are reviewing their child's case and invites them to be part of the process. There are a few cases where they would not send a letter to a family: for example, they do not always send one if the child was under a year old and died in natural circumstances in hospital and was never brought home, because the family is likely to have less to offer in these kinds of circumstances and sometimes the coroner has made a note that the family has requested no contact. A significant proportion of families do not respond to letters straight away.

'They may wait for the day when they feel they have enough inner strength or they feel today is the day they can speak about it, and when that happens we want to be able to respond to them on that day because the next day may not be a good day. We try wherever possible to be cognisant of anniversaries ... if I'm calling a family back I always check the file and check the date as it might be a significant date for that family.'

If a parent calls the call will be transferred to the person who was the primary reviewer on the case. Depending on what the parent wants, and where they live in the province (because reviewers' ability to travel has been reduced as a result of budget constraints), they may go and visit them or communicate by phone or email.

'It's very much in the hands of the parent to direct the amount that they want to interact with us and we give the control back to them.'

Reviewers report that they are able to obtain information from families that was not available in files.

'There's a lot to be learned from the family. We take a very ecological, holistic approach to it, much more public health than death investigation. We like to look at not necessarily what happened in the seconds before the child died but what it is that led the child, that culminated in the child being in a set of circumstances at that time, that s/he made that decision to drink alcohol or take their own life or whatever it was ...some of those you can't glean from a coroner's file because their investigation doesn't need to answer those questions.'

Parents may, for example, have spoken to their child's friends after the death and found out information that their child had not shared with them previously.

'I spoke to a father whose son died by suicide. The father spoke to me and told me his son's story and then he said I'm going to pass you over to his best friend, and the best friend told me a totally different story, most of which the father hadn't known about – criminality, drugs ... – and at the end he said I've never spoken about these things because it would have been disrespectful after he died ... Depending on the age of a child a parent either knows everything that's going on in a child's life or knows nothing.'

A quarter of cases reviewed in 2009 involved aboriginal children, but the review team report that they have traditionally had a low level of engagement with aboriginal families.

'There are some challenges being in the coroner's system and getting a letter from the coroner's service as opposed to getting a letter from public health ... particularly in our aboriginal population who don't tend to speak to government.'

They are endeavouring to strengthen relationships with aboriginal families. A masters student recently looked at this issue and made a number of recommendations to improve practice.

The CDR team examines aggregate case findings to identify trends or emergent issues that require targeted action and develops recommendations aimed at preventing similar deaths in the future. If further examination of an issue is required it can recommend that the chief coroner convenes a death review panel. CDR panels review the facts and circumstances of one or more deaths to provide advice and recommendations to the chief coroner that may impact public health and safety in the prevention of deaths. Individuals appointed to a panel may be content experts or may have an intimate understanding of the case under examination. CDR panels have been convened to examine the alcohol-related deaths of aboriginal youths, child and youth suicide deaths, drowning deaths, SIDs and child pedestrian deaths. Reviews always include the family's perspective and a review of best practices from other jurisdictions.

The CDR team also publishes special reports on specific issues that demand more in-depth analysis and targeted action. They have produced special reports on suicide and SUDI (Sudden Unexpected Deaths in Infants) deaths, looking at aggregated data over a number of years. The Safe and Sound report of SUDI deaths (CDRU, 2009) was triggered by a number of deaths in 2007 in a small geographical area. When the team started to look into this they realised there were preventable aspects to some of the deaths. They undertook a survey of stakeholders — of public health nurses, paediatricians, midwives and others to find out what people thought SUDI was, what they did in their practice and what they thought the messages should be. They received more than a thousand responses across the province. In order to assess what impact their prevention activity around safe sleeping had they sent a feedback form to all the original respondents a year later asking whether anything had changed in terms of programmes and policies and asking if they would be interested in attending a webinar on SUID.

BC has a separate process for reviewing deaths of children known to the child welfare service. The Office of the Representative for Children and Youth has a mandate to review the deaths and critical injuries of children in care of the Ministry of Children and Family Development (MCFD) and of children who were in receipt of reviewable services within twelve months of their death. The Hughes review had recommended this but also suggested that the function be reviewed after five years, by which time they expected the ministry would be strengthened and the CDR process would be operating. However, the process has recently been reviewed and is to continue.

The representative is an independent member of the legislature and has powers to obtain any information that is needed from any public body. This means that review of these cases is far more multi-disciplinary than it is in many other places that have internal review. Some police services are provided by the Royal Canadian Mounted Police, a federal agency not covered by BC legislation, but the representative has entered into an agreement with it to provide information.

> 'We've got pretty much unparalleled access to information and all of the information that we hold is protected by statute so nobody can get our records nor can they call any of us to serve as witnesses in court cases.'

There is a team of investigators for reviewing cases, and external expertise may be brought in to assist on specific cases: for example, someone with experience of domestic violence policy was recently brought in; medical expertise from a paediatrician is also hired in. Cases are presented to a multi-disciplinary advisory committee, which meets two or three times a year. Cases cannot be investigated until a year after the event and/or until a criminal investigation is complete. The process is more formal than in many other places.

> 'Investigations are conducted according to a public inquiry model if you take the word public out. They're not conducted in public but they are formal processes that require interviewing relevant people ... and we have powers to compel witnesses to appear and we compel every witness co-operative or not because that also protects the witness because it means what they have told us, the evidence that they have provided, can't be accessed so that helps deal with certain issues like retribution from the employer for things that you've said. We allow them to have legal counsel present but it's not for any cross examination kind of reason — they're just there for support and in case the individual

> wants some advice about responding … So we conduct our interviews quite formally. People are sworn in and give sworn evidence as if they are in a courtroom. We typically record them. We produce transcripts in order to verify what we're talking about.'

There is an administrative fairness procedure so people who may be affected or organisations that have been involved receive a confidential draft of reports and can respond to points of accuracy. Investigations are very resource-intensive and require a lot of time and travel. Recommendations are followed up, and written progress updates are requested. A select standing committee on children and youth receives the reports.

Families are involved in the process, and professionals report that this generates invaluable information and is important to families in terms of closure. Particular efforts are made to involve First Nation communities.

The Hughes review stressed the importance of aggregated reviews, and these are, therefore, undertaken to look at specific kinds of deaths or critical injuries. These reviews rely only on documents, and so far only one has been published, a review of twenty-one children under the age of two, which demonstrated that many families are living in extreme poverty. A second aggregate review of sixty-two suicide and self-harm cases has recently been completed.

Ontario

Since the 1990s CDR in Ontario has been undertaken by committees with dedicated funding, which are situated within the Office of the Chief Coroner; review is undertaken at provincial not local level. The coroner's system in Ontario is unusual in that all coroners are physicians. This is unique in North America. There are two separate review committees for reviewing child deaths — the Death Under Five Committee reviews all deaths of children under five that the coroner investigates; a separate Paediatric Death Review Committee examines medically complex deaths or cases where there are concerns regarding medical care, as well as all deaths of children where the family has a file open to a Children's Aid Society at the time of death, or within twelve months of death. Some cases may be subjected to both medical and child welfare review. About half of all deaths of children and young people under nineteen in Ontario are reviewed in total. Ontario is a large province, and professionals engaged in CDR believe it would not be possible to review all deaths in the province.

> 'If you're a local Child Death Review committee and have fifty deaths a year you can look at them all. Here we can't look at 600 deaths. We don't need to look at 600 deaths.'

The Paediatric Death Review Committee has been operating the longest. It was set up in 1995 and initially reviewed only complex medical cases. Child welfare cases were added following a child mortality task force in response to a number of homicides of children known to the child welfare service in the early 1990s and concern that no one was looking at these deaths. The task force reviewed around a hundred deaths. There has been a child welfare representative on the Paediatric Death Review Committee since the late 1990s, and the number of representatives from child welfare has grown over time to the current complement of five. The task force also recommended the establishment of the under-fives committee.

There are two streams of review for deaths of children under five. An executive committee composed of two physician reviewers examines straightforward accidental deaths from fire, drowning and other causes; it also reviews natural deaths, deaths of children known to a Children's Aid Society and complex medical care cases. It can shunt cases back to the bigger committee if necessary. The bigger committee includes forensic pathologists, police detectives, a child maltreatment specialist, an attorney and an epidemiologist/public health representative. Some 15–20 cases are reviewed each session from an oversight perspective to see whether pathology, the police or any other agency has missed anything. The information is also used to determine cause and manner of death by consensus decision. A report goes to the chief coroner, deputy chief coroners and ten regional supervising coroners. Public safety messages can come out of these reports: for example, on around safe sleeping.

The Paediatric Death Review Committee is made up of child welfare specialists, police officers, and paediatric specialists. It comprises a child welfare tract and a medical tract. The medical tract is for complex medical cases where the cause of death is uncertain or where there are issues around care. One expert does a case review, then there is a consensus conversation to come up with recommendations.

> 'The medical community listens to us because of our stature.'

For the child welfare deaths there is a joint directive with the children's ministry. The children's ministry report all cases to the Paediatric Death Review Committee, and it decides whether the agency should do an internal review. Reviews are undertaken in about 40% of cases. Internal reviews must include an external representative. Internal review reports get sent to the committee, and it reviews this as well as coroner's reports and police reports, and a report is sent back to the agency with recommendations. An annual report of cases reviewed over the year with recommendations is produced.

> 'The focus is supposed to be on prevention, and agencies are told that when they do their internal review it should be a non-blaming quality-assurance review with a goal of learning so things can be done differently and the same death won't happen again.'

Family involvement is minimal in Ontario. Families are made aware of under-fives reports and can obtain those. For child welfare reports the family may know there has been a review, but they do not get these reports.

> 'They're meant to be a quality-assurance report for the agencies; they're not meant to be used by families ... they're not really meant for public view.'

Because the CDR committees are located within the coroner's office they can obtain any records they need for the purpose of review. People involved in CDR in Ontario also report that being located in the coroner's office ensures that agencies are more willing to listen to their findings.

> 'We don't struggle in the same way that some teams do in terms of getting people to listen to us. I've heard people [in the US] saying that people don't read their reports and

> people don't want to hear what they have to say. People really anticipate our reports and the child welfare system here is a big important thing for them … I think part of it is because the coroner's office generally has authority and respect from the general public for the most part so I think we're fortunate to have our death review here because I think we do make a lot more headway than a lot of other jurisdictions.'

They concede, however, that the coroner's office is restricted in terms of being able to follow up on recommendations. They report that they have sometimes struggled to get their messages out but are working on effective ways of getting others to do this for them.

CONCLUSION

- There are no federal requirements to undertake CDR in the US or Canada. There is, therefore, no national co-ordination in the US or Canada, and states and provinces organise their CDR systems in different ways. Only one state in the US does not have CDR, but only a small number of Canadian provinces have CDR processes.
- Some states in the US have local review, some have state review, some have local and state review, some have state and regional review; review is only undertaken at provincial level in Canada.
- CDR is mandated in British Columbia and Ontario. In most US states CDR is rooted in legislation, but some states do not have legislation and in others legislation permits but does not mandate CDR.
- Review is funded in British Columbia and Ontario. The funding situation varies across the US. Some states have dedicated funding streams while others have no funding at all.
- The focus of review varies in the US, but most CDR teams now review all unexpected deaths and some review all deaths; British Columbia reviews all deaths, while review in Ontario is limited to children under five, medically complex deaths and deaths of children known to child protection agencies.
- Thirty-six US states use the NCCDR case reporting system, so some national data is available; national data is not available in Canada.
- Families are involved in CDR in British Columbia but not in Ontario. Families are not normally involved in the US.

CHAPTER 3

Child Death Review in England and Wales

Introduction

In the UK finding out what has happened when a child dies is a basic human right now enshrined in Articles 2 and 3 of the Human Rights Act 1998 (Rose and Barnes, 2008), and all parts of the UK have well-developed processes for reviewing deaths from abuse and neglect and other serious cases. These processes for reviewing serious cases vary in different parts of the UK (Vincent, 2010) but have the same overall purpose – to establish whether lessons can be learned from a case in terms of improving inter-agency working and better protecting children. Case reviews are not inquiries into how a child died or was seriously harmed, or into who is culpable. They are intended to be used as a learning tool, not as a means of attributing blame.

Until recently no parts of the UK had wider CDR processes equivalent to those in the US, New Zealand and some Canadian and Australian states. England (in 2008) and Wales (in 2009) introduced wider CDR processes, but these are quite different. Scotland and Northern Ireland do not have structures for wider review of child deaths, although new procedures are being developed in Northern Ireland. At the time of writing the Scottish government had not announced any plans to introduce new systems for wider review of child deaths as in England and Wales (Vincent, 2010; Stafford *et al.*, 2011). This chapter outlines the nationally co-ordinated, locally administered system of review that has been introduced in England. It also describes the new national review process that has been developed in Wales.

Table 3.1 Overview of CDR processes in England and Wales

Country	Key players	Legislation	Scope of review
England	Child Death Overview Panels (CDOPs) in Local Safeguarding Children's Boards (LSCBs)	Children Act 2004; Children and Young Persons Act 2008	All deaths 0–18
Wales	Child death panels, Public Health Wales	None	Cases are selected for review according to themes

ENGLAND

Since 1 April 2008 in an attempt to create a wider public health approach to understanding all child deaths, Local Safeguarding Children's Boards (LSCBs) in England have a statutory duty under the Children Act 2004 to:

- review all child deaths from birth to eighteen years old in a systematic way through a Child Death Overview Panel (CDOP) (excluding babies who are stillborn and planned terminations of pregnancy carried out within the law);
- respond rapidly to individual unexpected deaths of all children, not just those in contact with organisations responsible for safeguarding their welfare, in the local authority area, through a rapid response team (RRT).

Funding was provided for an initial three-year period. An unexpected death is defined as a death:

> ... which was not anticipated as a significant possibility 24 hours before the death or where there was a similarly unexpected collapse leading to or precipitating the events which led to the death (HM Government, 2006).

When children die unexpectedly they are now routinely taken to an Accident and Emergency department, where they are examined by a paediatrician. Multi-agency case review meetings are held for all unexpected deaths, and a home visit is undertaken in all cases where children die suddenly or unexpectedly.

CDOPs must prepare an annual report of information for the LSCB, which has a statutory responsibility to use the aggregated findings from all child deaths, collected according to a nationally agreed data set, to inform local strategic planning on how best to safeguard and promote the welfare of children in their area. The LSCB has responsibility for disseminating the lessons to be learned from the CDR process to all relevant organisations, ensuring that relevant findings inform the Children and Young People's Plan and acting on any recommendations to improve policy, professional practice and inter-agency working to safeguard and promote the welfare of children. The LSCB is also required to supply anonymised data on child deaths to the Department for Education, so that the department can commission research and publish nationally comparable analyses of these deaths.

The overall purpose of CDR processes in England is to understand why children die, so interventions can be put in place to protect other children and prevent future deaths. The CDOP review process is a paper-based review, using information available from those who were involved in the care of the child, both before and immediately after the death, as well as information from other sources including, in some cases, the coroner. CDOP co-ordinators report that they spend considerable time chasing information and that there are often gaps in information particularly in relation to fathers. Even though they have developed e-forms they still receive information in various formats, and not necessarily electronically. Guidance (HM Government, 2010) states that panels should have a fixed core membership but should have flexibility to co-opt other relevant professionals as and when appropriate. It also states that the CDOP should meet at regular intervals to discuss the appropriateness of the professionals' responses to each death of a child, their involvement before and at the time of the death, and relevant environmental, social, health and cultural aspects of each death, to ensure a thorough consideration of how such deaths might be prevented in the future. Panels should classify the cause of death, make a decision as to the preventability of the death, identify any modifiable factors, and consider any recommendations that may be made about actions that could be taken to prevent such deaths in the future; they should also identify to whom recommendations should be addressed.

Evidence from a pilot study to determine whether confidential enquiry methodology could be used to identify avoidable factors in child deaths, by the Confidential Enquiry into Maternal and Child Health (CEMACH) (Pearson, 2008), suggested that a public health approach might be a more effective way of learning than focusing only on abuse and neglect-related deaths. It concluded that half of the deaths that panels considered might have been avoided would not have been identified as 'unexpected' under the 'working together' definition for Serious Case Reviews (SCRs), highlighting the need to review all child deaths rather than just unexpected ones.

Chapter 7 of *Working Together to Safeguard Children* (HM Government, 2006) initially set out the new processes for reviewing child deaths, setting the scene for England to become the first country in the world to have national standards and procedures for the investigation and management of unexpected child deaths and for reviewing all deaths (Sidebotham *et al.*, 2008). The guidelines in *Working Together* were based on the findings of the Kennedy report into the management of SUDI (RCPATH/RCPCH, 2004), which was convened after three high-profile infant death prosecutions failed. The government announced it would set up these new processes in its response to the inquiry into the death of Victoria Climbie. Prior to these new processes it was likely that only a minority of child deaths received a post-mortem and an even smaller number were accorded a public inquest. This information was, however, not actually known, since a breakdown of figures was not available by age from the Registrar General's office. Figures are available in Northern Ireland, where only a fifth of child deaths receive a post-mortem and just 13% are subject to a public inquest (Bunting and Reid, 2005).

In July 2008, in partnership with the Ministry of Justice (MoJ), the Department for Children Schools and Families (DCSF) amended the Coroners Rules 1984 to place a duty on coroners to notify LSCBs of all child deaths over which they have jurisdiction. A power for coroners to provide LSCBs with information relevant to children who die and for whom they have jurisdiction was also introduced. With the enactment of the Children and Young Persons Act 2008, from 1 April 2009 registrars have a duty to provide LSCBs with the information on the child's death certificate. In addition, the Registrar General has a duty to provide the Secretary of State with information on all child deaths including those that occur abroad.

The public sector agreement to 'improve children and young people's safety' (HM Government, 2008) includes monitoring preventable child deaths as recorded through CDR panel processes (indicator 4), and LSCBs have to provide information to monitor the progress being made against this national indicator. From 1 April 2008 they had to collect information on the number of child deaths that had been reviewed by CDOPs, and the number of these cases that were assessed as being preventable child deaths. In July 2009 the DCSF published figures on child deaths for the first time, which showed that LSCBs in England reviewed 2,000 deaths between 1 April 2008 and 31

March 2009, of which 110 were considered to have been preventable (5%) (DCSF, 2009). Because this was the first year that child deaths had been reviewed and recorded, the DCSF warned, however, that the figures should be interpreted with caution. Not all deaths in 2008/9 had been fully reviewed on 31 March 2009 by their CDOP because of the time lag between the death and the assessment of the available information about the child death. Panels also reported that they had encountered a number of process issues that had further reduced the number of deaths they were able to review. The DCSF (2009) concluded that the completeness of the data provided would have been compromised in the following ways:

- Not all LSCBs had been informed of every child death within their area and therefore had not been able to review all deaths.
- Where incomplete information about the child had been provided to panels, they were not able to identify the child and therefore could not gather information to assess the death.
- Where panels experienced delays while waiting for post-mortem results, coroners' reports, criminal investigation outcomes and SCR outcomes they were unable to review some child deaths fully by 31 March 2009.
- Some LSCBs prioritised the order in which deaths were reviewed, due to the limited number of times the panels were able to meet before 31 March 2009. Some panels ensured that deaths where lessons needed to be learned were addressed first. This has resulted in a number of expected and probably unpreventable deaths yet to be reviewed on 31 March 2009.
- LSCBs reported difficulties in understanding and interpreting the definition of preventable child deaths, resulting in a number of panels failing to reach a decision on preventability for some of the most complex deaths by 31 March 2009.
- There were inconsistencies in how panels interpreted the guidance around the reviewing of all child deaths, with some panels reporting that they had not reviewed neonatal deaths or only reviewed unexpected deaths. Other panels felt that they were unable to review the deaths that occurred before the panels were set up, and chairs and co-ordinators were

recruited. In some LSCBs this has resulted in deaths for only a quarter of the year being considered by the panel.

Key changes in Chapter 7 of the updated *Working Together* (HM Government, 2010) included revised definitions of preventable child deaths and unexpected deaths and clarity on the roles of coroners and registrars and on how to respond appropriately to the deaths of children with life-limiting illnesses. There was also an additional section, which clarified the level of involvement of parents and other family members and the support they needed. The guidance stated:

> It is vitally important that LSCBs establish mechanisms for appropriately informing and involving parents and other family members in both the child death overview and the rapid response processes … The LSCB, acting through the CDOP, should agree what information is to be shared with parents and family members and ensure that a professional known to the family conveys to them agreed information in a sensitive and timely manner. Decisions on information sharing (i.e. what information is shared, with whom and why) must be recorded in each agency's records. It is not appropriate, however, for parents to attend the CDOP meeting as this is a meeting for professionals to discuss not only the individual case but also wider public health issues. Parents should, however, be encouraged to contribute any comments or questions they might have to the review of their child's death.
>
> Parents should be informed that all cases will be anonymised prior to discussion by the CDOP, information gathered will be stored securely and only anonymised data will be collated at a regional or national level. Parents should also be made aware that the CDOP will make recommendations and report on the lessons learned to the LSCB. The LSCB produces an annual report, which is a public document, but it will not contain any personal information that could identify an individual child or their family.
>
> CDOPs should ensure that, whenever necessary, arrangements are made for the family to have the opportunity to

meet with relevant professionals: for example, a professional known to the family before their child died, a paediatrician or a police officer to help answer their questions (HM Government, 2010).

CDOPs have designed information leaflets to give to families, but some people involved in CDR in England report that giving a leaflet to a parent whose child has just died can be a 'cold approach' and it may be better to talk things through with families. Some LSCBs have, therefore, recruited bereavement nurses to liaise with parents.

Some 3,450 child death reviews were completed by CDOPs in the year ending 31 March 2010, and 150 were assessed as preventable (Department for Education, 2010). In 2009/10 LSCBs were also asked to provide additional voluntary information about the child deaths they had reviewed — for example, details about the child's age, gender, ethnicity and cause of death — and this data was provided on behalf of 123 out of the 145 LSCBs. This voluntary data indicated that:

- the majority of deaths assessed as preventable were due to trauma and other external factors (54%)
- 27% were due to road traffic accidents; 15% to other events and 13% to other non-intentional injury, accidents or trauma;
- 27% of deaths assessed as preventable were for children aged 1–4 years; 26% for children aged 15–17 years; and 19% for children aged 10–14 years.

Since not all LSCBs provided data the Department for Education (2010) warned, however, that the figures did not accurately reflect national proportions and should be treated with caution. For 2010/11 LSCBs were required to provide this information at aggregate level. A number of people involved in CDR in LSCBs in England have reported that they are disappointed with the extent to which the data has been used at national level.

> 'Far more could be done with the national data. We're sitting on lots of unused data. We have so much information'

The pilot study by Sidebotham *et al.* (2008) provided some evidence of how the new CDR processes were operating in England. Nine

LSCBs that responded to an initial questionnaire were selected as sites for further research. CDOPs were at an early stage of development when the pilot study was undertaken, but a number of outcomes were already being observed, such as public awareness campaigns, community safety initiatives, training of professionals, development of protocols and lobbying of politicians.

Although the Sidebotham *et al.* (2008) study provided some evidence of the effectiveness of new CDR processes it also identified a number of problems. One of the main ones was that none of the nine overview panels in the pilot had managed to set up a foolproof system of notification. Most sites commented that current systems for notification of deaths were inadequate and that they had to rely on a combination of sources: child surveillance teams or decision support teams of the Primary Care Trusts; coroners; the police; children's social care; public health; hospital records departments; and registrars. Notification of deaths of children who lived in one area but who died outside this area was particularly problematic. One LSCB reported that they received notifications of all child deaths from a tertiary hospital in their area regardless of the child's place of residence.

These concerns could prove to be significant, since evidence suggests that 40% of deaths of children under one and between a quarter and a third of deaths of older children occur outside the area in which the child resided, making local ascertainment of death problematic (Ward Platt, 2007). New duties on coroners to notify LSCBs of all deaths were designed to address these problems and have ensured that the notification process is more straightforward. *Working Together* stated: 'The CDOP should have a clear relationship and agreed channels of communication with the local coronial service' (HM Government, 2010). However, while some CDOPs report that they have good relationships with coroners, others state that they have somewhat tense relationships with coroners, who do not always recognise the benefits of the CDR process.

Participants in the Sidebotham *et al.* (2008) study cited various systems for review of children's deaths — local case discussions for SUDI; local case discussions for other unexpected child deaths; infant mortality reviews in hospital and by the perinatal unit; other hospital mortality reviews and domestic violence reviews — but reported that there was not a consistent process. The nine sites all had protocols for responding to unexpected childhood deaths, many of which had been operational for several years, but most covered only unexpected deaths of children under two. There were some concerns about reviewing all deaths of 0–18 year olds, particularly in relation to the neonatal period and later adolescent period, since different professionals were involved with the older and younger age group. In many sites there was already some sort of hospital-based neonatal mortality review, and the challenge was to try to include them in the CDOP process rather than replace an already well-functioning system.

As in some other countries some CDOPs divide deaths into categories and review all deaths within one category at a time to enable appropriate expertise to be brought in to support the panel. While there was a general sense of enthusiasm for developing CDR processes there was some frustration at the perceived lack of central guidance other than that set out in *Working Together* (HM Government, 2006). As a result in 2008 the DCSF made available a training resource to support LSCBs in implementing the CDR processes set out in Chapter 7 of *Working Together*.

Chapter 7 of *Working Together* (HM Government, 2006) required LSCBs to establish CDOPs for populations greater than 500,000 and stated that neighbouring LSCBs could form combined CDOPs to achieve this population size. Some LSCBs — for example, Wolverhampton and Walsall in the West Midlands — have a combined CDOP. Sidebotham *et al.* (2008) found that some panels were planning to develop a combined CDOP, while others were not keen to do so even where population numbers were low. They found that teams could function with both smaller and larger populations and concluded that LSCBs should consider what configuration best met their needs. Ward Platt (2007) commented, however, that from his experience in the north of England (a participating region in the CEMACH child death project) it made sense for adjacent LSCBs to pool expertise and cover larger populations than their own. He suggested that populations of between 500,000 and a million would allow a reasonable number of deaths to be scrutinised each year without the process becoming too onerous.

In London a CDOP Chairs' Group has been established to:

- support London CDOP chairs to undertake their role and the functions of their panels;
- promote a consistent high quality of child death response and review across London.

This provides peer challenge and support for chairs and is a good way of identifying and sharing good practice in terms of multi-agency responses to child deaths across London. London-wide annual reports are produced, and child death data is collated and analysed for the whole of London.

Similar groups have been established in other parts of the country: for example, a West Midlands regional group meets periodically to share information and develop regional prevention initiatives. The group has looked at SUDI deaths and will now look at life-limiting conditions. The group recently analysed data across the region. This process highlighted that different CDOPs do things differently: for example, in some cases ethnicity was listed as unknown.

The *Working Together* guidance (HM Government, 2006) included a diagram to explain the interface between child death and SCR processes, but Sidebotham *et al.* (2008) found there were problems around linkage of the two processes. There was a clear message from interviewees that SCRs were intensive, demanding and time-consuming and that SCR processes could not, and should not, go into the same kind of depth. Participants were also unclear about the distinction between child death overview processes and rapid response processes. They talked about the differences between the multi-agency child death overview and other hospital-based mortality reviews, which were already being undertaken in many places, and generally considered that the CDOP should consider cases only after the conclusion of any rapid response process, criminal investigation or SCR. The updated Chapter 8 guidance (HM Government, 2010) provided more information on the interface between the separate processes for reviewing child deaths.

Early evidence suggests that CDR procedures in England are beginning to lead to positive prevention initiatives. The Department for Education (2010) statistical release included a list of actions that LSCBs have taken following reviews of child deaths:

- awareness campaigns around safe sleeping to reduce the

number of SIDs and deaths related to sleeping in parents' beds or on the sofa with parents;

- making improvements to local roads, including traffic-calming measures, cycle lanes and barriers, parking restrictions, warning signs and reducing foliage, as well as introducing additional road safety training for school children, to reduce the number of deaths caused by traffic accidents;
- running community road shows to share a range of findings from child death reviews;
- making sure leaflets are available in more languages, especially around safe sleeping for babies;
- reviewing how children who present at Accident and Emergency departments because of apparent self-harm are assessed and monitored;
- reviewing procedures following non-attendance at health appointments, including vaccinations;
- raising awareness of the dangers of leaving children unattended in the bath — whether in a bath seat or not;
- reviewing services available to children, ranging from advice on pregnancy and sexual health to accessibility of services for re-housed families with disabled children or children with life-limiting illnesses;
- contacting GPs to ensure that databases are up to date so that end-of-life plans are accurate and can be shared with other services, such as ambulance services;
- reviewing the bereavement support offered to families;
- offering feedback to services including recognising good practice and sharing with others;
- providing awareness-raising campaigns around securing disabled children's wheelchairs in vehicles;
- reviewing psychological support for children with chronic conditions, namely epilepsy and diabetes;
- obtaining information on research and work being conducted around the UK where children from consanguineous parents die;
- producing leaflets warning of the dangers of air weapons, and displaying these in hospitals, police stations and schools.

WALES

The Welsh regulations under the Children Act 2004 did not require individual LSCBs in Wales to review all child deaths or to respond rapidly to individual unexpected deaths of all children as they did in England. Because the population base of LSCBs in Wales was significantly less than the recommended 500,000 for CDR arrangements in England, the Welsh Assembly government chose instead to investigate whether an all-Wales approach would be a more feasible way of administering child death reviews, and they commissioned the National Public Health Service for Wales to undertake a pilot study of the practicality of this. The pilot began in July 2009 and was expected to run for a year, resulting in a report for the Welsh Assembly government on how the CDR process should be taken forward in Wales. The pilot concentrated on three tasks:

- ascertaining all child deaths (0–<18 years) from 1 October 2009 until the end of the pilot;
- establishing national reviews of deaths, initially focusing on suicides and apparent suicides since 1 October 2006;
- testing the feasibility of establishing local reviews/case discussions and integrating completion of information requirements into current processes.

The pilot was expected to result in surveillance of all childhood deaths in Wales, underpinned by a child death database and by review of unexpected child deaths, as in England. It soon became obvious that this would not be feasible within a year, and in 2011 the Welsh Assembly government announced that the CDR pilot would be extended for a further year and that an independent evaluation would be commissioned to explore the structures and processes to ensure that they were effective. Funding has now been provided to continue CDR for another two years.

CDR in Wales was introduced following a review of the SUDI protocol. The review found that the protocol was not fit for purpose because it covered only deaths up to age two whereas unexpected deaths should be reviewed up to age eighteen. The *Procedural Response to Unexpected Deaths in Childhood (PRUDiC)* document stated that if a child aged 0–18 dies unexpectedly the police should be involved and the body should be taken to an Accident and Emergency department not to a mortuary and be seen by a paediatric consultant (Wood and Naughton, 2010). This is similar to the rapid response process in England. Wales were unable to establish RRTs as in England but developed PRUDiC practitioners instead. The PRUDiC practitioner can be any professional but has to be someone close to the family. For all cases of unexpected child deaths the police, the PRUDiC practitioner and the paediatrician have a discussion and decide whether they need to visit the home. They may hold a PRUDiC meeting of all professionals who had contact with the child.

Wales have had a national database of all child deaths since October 2009. It holds information on all deaths of children aged 0–18. The child has to have taken a breath — stillborn deaths are not included. Some 250–300 deaths a year meet the criteria. Not all deaths are reviewed. Different types of deaths are examined by thematic panels, which recommend prevention initiatives: for example, suicide deaths have been reviewed. The composition of panels varies according to what deaths are being investigated but may comprise representatives from child health, education, police, public health, social services, Children in Wales and the Children's Commissioner.

The CDR co-ordinator receives notifications of deaths from the PRUDiC practitioner along with basic demographic details of the child, and data relating to the death such as where it occurred, and what type of death it was. The main types of death are categorised as: suicide; drowning; homicide; fire; poisoning; motor vehicle accidents (broken down into those in which the child was the driver, the passenger, a pedestrian or involved in a cycle accident); life-limiting conditions; medical deaths that are not life-limiting; infant deaths; and neonatal deaths. Neonatal deaths are not reviewed because the perinatal survey does this and the CDR team does not want to duplicate this. The co-ordinator also receives information on all registered deaths from the Office of National Statistics (ONS). The national database is automatically uploaded with information from ONS, but it can take two years for information to be inputted.

If children who are normally resident in Wales die outside of Wales the CDR co-ordinator is notified and these deaths will be included. If a child dies in England the co-ordinator receives reports from the LSCB and health authority. If the child dies in Wales but does not normally reside in Wales the death will not be included in the total number of child deaths in Wales, but information on these deaths will be stored and can be used to inform thematic reviews: for example, if a child who did not reside in Wales died on a particularly dangerous road it is useful to include information about their death to inform prevention activity.

One of the problems with the Welsh data system is that rather than developing their own data forms the Welsh adopted the forms that were being used in England, which were not necessarily suitable for the Welsh context, not least because reviews are not undertaken on every death at local level as they are in England: 'The Child Death Overview Panels in England have greater resources at their disposal and the process in England is not directly translatable to a Welsh context' (Welsh Government, 2012).

The evaluation of the CDR pilot in Wales concluded that the forms were over-ambitious in that they were aiming to ascertain too much detailed information that agencies did not necessarily hold. The forms are now being adapted so that the CDR co-ordinator will collect and record only demographic data on the child death database, which will be obtained from ONS and supplemented from details gained from the Welsh Paediatric Surveillance Unit and other sources. Further contextual information will be collected only if a death is to be reviewed by the thematic panels. In-depth information will, therefore, be garnered on only a small number of children, but there will be a core dataset of information for all deaths that can be used to produce an annual report.

The CDR process in Wales is not underpinned by legislation, and information sharing has been problematic as a result. One of the reasons why the pilot was extended was because it took longer to obtain information than had been anticipated. LSCBs were expected to provide information but they were often the last to know about child deaths. Information is rarely obtained from coroners, although some individual coroners have been helpful. Information on children can be obtained because there are no data protection issues around this data, but gathering information about parents and siblings has been more difficult. Family information is requested for all SIDs deaths because such information is particularly useful for these types of deaths and is crucial, for example, in relation to establishing the facts in relation to co-sleeping. While the police are usually willing to provide third-party information, health services are not.

> The Child Death Review pilot project encountered some difficulty in locating and accessing data. This was due to data about child deaths being held by a wide range of organisations, and reluctance by some organisations to share information due to concerns about data protection (Welsh Government, 2012).

The independent evaluation of the CDR process did not recommend the introduction of a statutory framework for CDR in Wales but concluded that further consideration be given to the possibility of statutory powers in relation to the collection of and access to data because the CDR team had to have the right to request and access information from all agencies including social care, health, police and coroners. It will be interesting to see whether legislation is introduced around this in the new Social Services Bill in Wales.

When setting up their new CDR system Wales considered models in other countries and based their thematic reviews on those undertaken in NSW in Australia. It was initially hoped that thematic reviews could be undertaken quarterly, but it became obvious that this was over-ambitious. It can be time-consuming to undertake thematic reviews and, unlike in NSW where a dedicated review team exists to undertake themed reviews, in Wales there is only one CDR co-ordinator to do this and they also have responsibility for maintaining the national database. It is also particularly difficult to undertake these kinds of reviews when the CDR system is so new.

Because the CDR process was established only in 2009 there was insufficient data in the national database on which to base thematic reviews. They could be undertaken only by going back further than 2009, meaning the co-ordinator spent a long time chasing data. As seen in Chapter 1 people involved in CDR in New Zealand felt they only had sufficient numbers of deaths in their database to identify trends over time and to undertake thematic reviews after seven years of operation. Because of the small number of deaths in Wales it may be more useful to produce data reports every three or five years — as some smaller teams have done in the US — rather than produce annual reports.

A suicide review and co-sleeping one have now been undertaken in Wales, and a thematic examination of motor vehicle deaths of children aged thirteen to eighteen over a five-year period is now being undertaken. However, review reports are not released publicly. In order to undertake thematic reviews the co-ordinator looks at police reports, then may request social care reports and other information.

CDR in Wales arguably has the potential to be more public health and prevention focused than in England, because the function is situated within Public Health Wales rather than in LSCBs. However, some of the professionals who participated in the evaluation of the pilot project commented that review panels were too health focused and should be more balanced to include a wider range of professional perspectives. In addition, small numbers of deaths in Wales make the public health fit problematic, because public health will not release information when numbers are so small. Taking the recommendations from thematic panels forward has also been a challenge.

> We believe it is necessary to ensure that the Child Death Review process does not end with the production of reports. Instead we suggest that the Terms of Reference include a specific focus on the development and dissemination of robust and relevant recommendations, in order for the process to continue and have a real impact (Welsh Government, 2012).

Because the CDR process is not rooted in legislation panels have no powers to follow up on recommendations. LSCBs are multi-agency and, therefore, would seem to be the most obvious group to take forward recommendations, but despite a broadening of focus in recent years LSCBs can still be fairly child protection focused, which some would argue is appropriate (Vincent, 2010). People who participated in the evaluation of the pilot felt that dissemination of recommendations was not necessarily a task for the CDR panel and that recommendations should be developed in conjunction with agencies such as the Welsh government or Public Health Wales who might have greater influence over implementation.

Because the CDR process is not situated within LSCBs there are issues around the link between CDR and SCR in Wales. The CDR co-ordinator needs access to SCR reports and information from SCRs, but there has been no national database of SCRs in Wales. Furthermore, LSCBs have not provided CDR with any information on SCRs, and although executive summaries are published they are completely anonymised so data from reports cannot be used for CDR purposes.

Families have not really been involved in the CDR process in Wales. A leaflet is given to families informing them of the process, and telling them how it works and why information is needed. It also tells families they can contact the CDR team if they wish. The PRUDiC practitioner has a lot of involvement with families, and individuals involved in CDR felt that if families were also told about CDR and perhaps SCRs as well this may be overwhelming.

REVIEW OF CASES WHERE ABUSE AND NEGLECT ARE SUSPECTED IN ENGLAND AND WALES

England and Wales have separate review processes for cases where abuse and neglect are suspected. Case review processes were introduced in both countries in 1991 under the *Working Together* under the Children Act 1989 guidelines (Home Office *et al.*, 1991). The introduction of case review processes was a deliberate move away from the type of large-scale, inquisitorial-style inquiries that characterised the 1980s. The government could still order a public inquiry after 1991, but did so only in exceptional circumstances: for example, following the death of Victoria Climbie (Corby *et al.*, 2001; Sinclair and Bullock, 2002; Corby, 2003). The guidance introduced a new process by which Area Child Protection Committees (ACPCs) would undertake Part 8 reviews (later known as Serious Case Reviews) in cases where children had been fatally abused, or abused with serious physical and psychological consequences. Local authorities were expected to inform the Department of Health of every case that was subject to a case review and could make their reports public if they considered there was sufficient public concern about the case. The guidelines were revised in England in the 1999 version of *Working Together to Safeguard Children* (Department of Health, Home Office, Department for Education and Employment,

1999), when the term 'serious case review' was first introduced, and in 2000 in Wales when the National Assembly produced *Safeguarding Children* (Welsh Assembly Government, 2006), its own version of *Working Together to Safeguard Children*.

The Children Act 2004 and its accompanying regulations placed SCRs on a statutory footing in England and Wales, and it is now mandatory for LSCBs, which replaced ACPCs, to conduct a SCR if a child dies and abuse or neglect is suspected to be a factor in the death. Whereas ACPCs were responsible for *monitoring* the process of case review SCR has now become a *function* of LSCBs (Brandon *et al.*, 2008; Rose and Barnes, 2008). The criteria for determining when a SCR should be undertaken were broadened. Until 2004 SCRs typically focused on deaths from severe physical assault or extreme neglect, but they now include suicide, deaths related to domestic violence incidents, deaths of children by a parent with a mental illness, and other deaths related to but not directly caused by maltreatment (Brandon *et al.*, 2008; Rose and Barnes, 2008).

Lord Laming (2009) in *The Protection of Children in England: A Progress Report* made a number of recommendations to strengthen and clarify the SCR process in England:

- The DCSF should revise *Working Together to Safeguard Children* so that it is explicit that the formal purpose of SCRs is to learn lessons for improving individual agencies as well as for improving multi-agency working.
- The DCSF should revise the framework for SCRs to ensure that the SCR panel chair has access to all of the relevant documents and staff they need to conduct a thorough and effective learning exercise.
- The DCSF should revise *Working Together to Safeguard Children* to ensure SCRs focus on the effective learning of lessons and implementation of recommendations and the timely introduction of changes to protect children.
- The DCSF should revise *Working Together to Safeguard Children* to underline the importance of a high-quality, publicly available executive summary, which accurately represents the full report, contains the action plan in full and includes the names of the SCR panel members.

- LSCBs should ensure all SCR review panel chairs and overview authors are independent of the LSCB and all services involved in the case and that arrangements for the SCR offer sufficient scrutiny and challenge.

Laming's (2009) recommendations were accepted by the then Labour government and new statutory guidance to replace Chapter 8 of *Working Together* was introduced with immediate effect in December 2009. The only one of Lord Laming's recommendations that was not taken forward entirely was that executive summaries should include the names of SCR panel members. Following consultation, it was agreed that executive summaries should include the job titles of panel members but not their names.

In 2007 responsibility for evaluating the quality of SCRs in England transferred to Ofsted from the Commission for Social Care Inspection. LSCBs were required to send completed SCR reports to Ofsted, which evaluated them against a set of grade descriptors and in accordance with an evaluation template. It assessed the extent to which the review fulfilled its purpose by reviewing the involvement of agencies, the rigour of analysis and the capacity for ensuring that the lessons identified were learned. Reports were graded as 'outstanding', 'good', 'adequate' or 'inadequate'. The outcome of the evaluation formed part of the evidence used for Ofsted's wider evaluation of the effectiveness of children's services in a local area. Inspection of review reports is unusual. Other countries, particularly Australia, often have second-tier oversight arrangements in place, but the only other place to have any kind of comparable system where individual review reports are inspected against a set of review criteria is Queensland. The Ofsted process was the subject of much criticism, for example:

> No attention, however, is being paid to what makes a good quality serious case review process. There is nothing in the grade descriptors used by Ofsted that would indicate any thinking has been done about either the methods by which a serious case review should be carried out, or the areas of academic research and discussion which might be relevant (Owen, 2009, p. 267).

Lord Laming included a recommendation that Ofsted should in future 'focus its evaluation of serious case reviews on the depth of learning a review has provided and the quality of the recommendations it has made to protect children' (Laming, 2009). His report suggested that Ofsted evaluations should focus on the:

- quality of the process of the review;
- adequacy of learning and change;
- professional practice;
- quality of the recommendations in protecting children to ensure that they are actively driving improved outcomes and better safeguarding systems (Laming, 2009).

Ofsted developed a revised evaluation framework for SCRs in response to Laming's recommendations, but their evaluations continued to be criticised. Participants in the Sidebotham *et al.* (2010) study reported overwhelmingly that Ofsted evaluations had resulted in too much emphasis on getting the process right rather than on improving outcomes for children. While Sidebotham *et al.*, (2010) concluded that Ofsted evaluations had led to an improvement in the overall quality of SCRs they recommended that reports should no longer be graded.

Since 2004 an independent author for the SCR overview report has been a requirement. Interestingly, however, Ofsted (2008) found there was no correlation between the quality of the overview report and the independence of its author. Laming (2009) commented that there was a lack of clarity around independence in the 2006 Chapter 8 guidance (HM Government, 2006) and the updated Chapter 8 guidance (HM Government, 2010) offered more clarity around this.

Sinclair and Bullock's (2002) analysis of SCRs was critical of the fact that families were excluded from the SCR process. As a result the 2006 Chapter 8 guidance (HM Government, 2006) required agencies to consider not just whether, but how, family members should be involved. New Welsh Guidance published in the same year (Welsh Assembly Government, 2006) also stated that the review panel should consider how family members could contribute to the review and who should be responsible for facilitating their involvement. In their analysis of SCRs Rose and Barnes (2008) found that family members had contributed in a fifth of cases. They stated, however, that this may not have been the full picture, since family members may have declined an invitation to contribute, the circumstances of the case may have made it inappropriate for them to contribute or the report may not have recorded discussions or negotiations about family involvement. Families were involved in nine out of forty-seven of the cases studied in depth by Brandon *et al.* (2008), and in a small number of cases the child also contributed. Ofsted (2008) found little evidence that agencies were working with families when undertaking SCRs:

- Eight out of fifty of the case reviews they evaluated recorded that families made a contribution.
- A further eight noted that families were invited to contribute but declined.
- In nineteen case reviews the issue was not covered at all.
- In eleven there was a statement that family members were not involved.
- A positive decision not to involve family members was noted in three reviews.

As part of their second evaluation of SCRs, Ofsted (2009) visited ten LSCBs whose SCRs had been evaluated as good. They found there was a more concerted effort to involve families in these LSCBs. In some cases families were contacted at an early stage of the review process and there were offers to meet family members on more than one occasion. The updated version of the Chapter 8 guidance (HM Government, 2010) stated that as well as involving family members the SCR panel should also make arrangements to provide feedback and debriefing to the child (if surviving) and family members/carers, following completion of the executive summary.

The Sidebotham *et al.* (2010) study found that family involvement remained problematic. Participants felt it was important for the family and community to be involved, but they were not clear about the purpose of engagement and felt there was no clear view as to whether families and communities could or should be holding agencies to account. Morris *et al.* (forthcoming) were recently funded by the British Association for the Study and Prevention of Child Abuse and Neglect (BASPCAN) to undertake a study of family involvement in reviews. The study considered local and national policy and procedures in relation to family involvement across the UK. It includes the experiences of families who have been involved in reviews and outlines the views of professionals around family involvement.

National analysis of SCRs

There have been attempts to learn from SCRs at national as well as local level through collation of findings in both England and Wales. In the 1990s three studies collated data from SCRs in England (Falkov, 1996; Reder *et al.*, 1993; Reder and Duncan, 1999). More recently, to try and bring clear standards and more consistent approaches to the case review process, the findings of SCRs in England have been collated in biennial analyses, which draw out key findings and assess their implications for policy and practice locally and nationally. The first of these biennial reviews by Sinclair and Bullock was published in 2002; and there have been further reviews by Rose and Barnes (2008) and Brandon *et al.* (2008; 2009).

Sidebotham *et al.* (2010) undertook a scoping exercise to develop recommendations on how to improve national approaches to learning from SCRs. Participants who took part in the study were clear that the system of national collation of SCRs generated useful information and could influence policy and practice. Sidebotham *et al.* (2010) recommended a revised system of national analysis. They suggested a research team should be commissioned for at least five years to provide an observatory/reporting function on all SCRs. The team would report annually on the numbers, patterns and key learning from SCRs, compare the findings with data from other sources and have responsibility for reviewing any national implications of recommendations from SCRs. Sidebotham *et al.* (2010) also recommended the establishment of a national steering group whose role would include recommending specific themes for analysis.

A number of analyses of SCRs have also been commissioned to inform policy in Wales (Owers *et al.*, 1999; Brandon *et al.*, 2002; Morris *et al.*, 2007). Depending on the number of SCRs they receive, the Welsh Assembly government has undertaken to commission overview reports every two years to draw out key findings and consider their implications for policy and practice. Marian Brandon and colleagues from the University of East Anglia recently completed a fourth analysis of SCRs in Wales which has not yet been published.

Recent SCR changes in England

There have been a number of recent changes around SCRs in England. In May 2010 the Coalition government announced that they were committed to publishing SCR de-identified overview reports as well as executive summaries. In June 2010 it sent a letter to LSCB chairs and directors of children's services informing them of a change to the statutory guidance set out in Chapter 8 of *Working Together* relating to publication of SCRs. From 10 June 2010 local authorities were to publish SCR overview reports 'unless there were compelling reasons relating to the welfare of any child directly concerned in the case for this not to happen'. The government outlined that the aim of this policy change was to restore public confidence and improve transparency in the child protection system, and ensure the context in which the events occurred was properly understood so lessons could be learned. The letter also announced that Eileen Munro had been appointed to undertake a review to improve child protection and that part of her remit would be to consider how SCRs could be strengthened.

Munro's (2011) review of child protection in England aimed to reduce the burden of inspection in England. It recommended that Ofsted no longer evaluate SCRs, but that the quality of learning more generally be given greater coverage within the overall inspection process. The review considered the:

- establishment of a national training programme in the systems approach and research methods;
- creation of a central pool of reviewers to support local areas;
- benefits of a national arbiter for case review standards and methods;
- creation of a standardised typology for presentation of findings;
- whether there was a basis to revise criteria for initiating SCRs.

It also considered the establishment of a national body, similar to the National Patient Safety Agency, to support national and local learning, train reviewers to conduct SCRs, provide quality assurance and collate findings of reviews to enable national learning. The review appeared to support the publication of overview reports. Munro (2011) admitted the policy has caused concern in relation to identification, but argued that by adopting systems methodology, with its focus on understanding why professionals acted as they did, it would be possible to write up and publish reviews with a focus on professional practice rather than on the detailed story of the child and family.

New arrangements in Wales

Until 2009 Wales had similar processes for reviewing cases where abuse and neglect were suspected as England. There were some differences — for example, SCRs in Wales were never graded by inspection teams — but it was not until 2009 that policy in Wales began to diverge markedly from that in England (Vincent, 2010; Stafford *et al.*, 2011). In 2009 Care and Social Services Inspectorate Wales (CSSIW) commissioned a review of the arrangements for conducting SCRs in Wales and their effectiveness in improving practice and inter-agency working. As in England, there had been a significant increase in the number of SCRs being undertaken by LSCBs, and the review suggested this provided further evidence of the fact that current review arrangements were not working effectively:

> There are fundamental questions being asked, therefore, about the ability of Serious Case Reviews, as currently constituted, to be the best vehicles for learning lessons when things have gone wrong and for improving safeguarding practice. There is a strange paradox that the greater the number of Serious Case Reviews undertaken, the weaker their impact seems to become (CSSIW, 2009, p. 3).

The review found there was a high level of agreement across Wales about shortcomings in the present arrangements and the reasons for them, which limited the effectiveness and impact of SCRs:

> There needs to be a more coherent and comprehensive LSCB framework for reviewing, learning and improving safeguarding practice which does not rely solely on serious case reviews as the driver for achieving change in policy (CSSIW, 2009, p. 3).

The review recommended a continuum of reviewing, learning and improving policy and practice. CSSIW (2009) commented that a new continuum approach could fit well with the overall development of work on CDR in Wales, although as we have seen there are some problems between the two processes. The Deputy Minister for Social Services, in a statement to the National Assembly on 20 October 2009, welcomed the report and its recommendations and asked for specific proposals for implementing the ideas in the report, so a second phase of work on next steps was commissioned in January 2010 with the purpose of developing proposals and guidance for implementation. A progress report by Wendy Rose — *Improving Practice to Protect Children in Wales: Developing a New National Framework for Learning and Reviewing* — was published in September 2010 and set out the broad direction of travel. The framework consists of:

- *Multi-agency professional forums*: an LSCB annual programme of multi-professional learning events for practitioners or managers, primarily to examine multi-agency case practice and findings from child protection audits, inspections and reviews to improve local knowledge and practice and to inform the board's future audit and training priorities.
- *Concise reviews*: a multi-agency review of practice in circumstances where a child has died or has been or was in danger of being seriously harmed as the result of abuse or neglect and was not on the child protection register within the last six months and was not a looked after child or a care leaver under the age of eighteen. The review engages with relevant children and families in so far as appropriate and seeks to include their perspectives, and it involves practitioners and their managers who have been working with the child and family. A planned and facilitiated practitioner-focused learning event is held, conducted by a reviewer independent of the case management, to examine recent practice using a systems approach. At the conclusion of the review there is an anonymised child practice review report, which is to be submitted to the Welsh government and published by the LSCB. The process is to be completed as soon as possible but no more than six months from a referral from the Board to the Review Sub-Group.

- *Extended reviews*: a multi-agency review where a child has died or has been or was in danger of being seriously harmed as a result of abuse or neglect and was on the child protection register within the last six months or was a looked after child or a care leaver under the age of eighteen. It follows the same process and timescale as a concise review, engaging with relevant children and families, in so far as they wish and is appropriate, and involving practitioners and managers throughout. There is an additional level of scrutiny of the work of the statutory agencies and the statutory plan(s) in place for the child or young person. The review is to be undertaken by two reviewers working closely together, one of whom will bring an external perspective and who will have responsibility for the scrutiny of how the statutory duties of all relevant agencies were fulfilled. An anonymised child practice review report is to be submitted to the Welsh government and published by the LSCB (Welsh Government, 2011).

The Rose (2010) report pointed out that the new framework of learning and review would have a number of implications, including the need: to review the role of policy and inspectorates in the new process; to seek compatibility with other related review systems; to amend existing regulations and guidance; to consider the resource consequences of the proposals; and to ensure an effective quality-assurance system is in place to test whether the intended benefits are being achieved.

> 'What is agreed is that this is not a technical exercise to replace one system, no longer fit for purpose, with another but that developing a national multi-agency approach for reviewing, learning and improving child protection practice will require wider and more far reaching changes in culture, systems and practice.'

The progress report was endorsed by the Welsh Safeguarding Children Forum, and in February 2011 the Welsh Assembly government announced plans to implement a new learning framework to replace SCRs. Draft practice guidance (Welsh Government, 2011) has been subject to national consultation. During 2012 pilot child practice reviews have been undertaken in accordance with the guidance to inform the detail of the new arrangements. Regulations regarding the responsibilities of LSCBs are being amended, and implementation of the new framework will commence in 2013.

CONCLUSION

- England has a mandated, nationally co-ordinated local CDR process that reviews all deaths.
- Wales has a government-funded, national review system. The system is not rooted in legislation, and not all deaths are reviewed. Themes are selected for review and all cases relating to that theme are examined.
- All local teams in England provide data to central government, so national data is now held on all children who have died. In Wales there is also a national database, which includes information on the deaths of all children and young people up to eighteen years.
- There is an expectation that families will be involved in the review process in England; families are not normally involved in Wales.

CHAPTER 4

Cross-country comparison of child death review processes

Introduction

CDR teams in Australia, New Zealand, North America and the UK are generally made up of a multi-agency group of experts, often specified in legislation, who meet regularly to review and discuss child deaths (Hochstadt, 2006). As the previous three chapters have shown, however, the ways in which teams are organised, what cases they review and how they perform their reviews varies widely within, as well as across, countries. Drawing on information presented in Chapters 1–3 this chapter offers a cross-country comparison of CDR processes. It outlines similarities and differences across countries, states and provinces in relation to legislation, focus of review, funding, family involvement and data. Key differences are:

- whether review is undertaken at state, local or national level;
- whether review has a legislative basis;
- where the review function is located and who undertakes the reviews;
- the focus of review – all deaths of children of all ages, or more restricted: for example, deaths from abuse and neglect; or deaths of children known to the child protection system;
- whether there is dedicated funding for review;
- whether families are involved in the review process;
- the availability and quality of data.

Table 4.1 Overview of approaches

Australia	Each state/territory is different. Some states do not have a CDR system. Review is at state level only. Location varies across states — the Children's Commissioner's office or Ombudsman's office is most common.
New Zealand	There is a national co-ordinated system of local review. CDR is situated within health.
USA	There is some degree of national co-ordination but each state is different: some have state review only; some county review only; some both. Location varies but generally there has been a move away from child welfare/justice towards public health.
Canada	Each province/territory is different. Some provinces do not have CDR systems. Review is at provincial level only. The CDR function is located in the coroner's office.
UK	Each part of the UK is different: England has a nationally co-ordinated system of local review within LSCBs; Wales has a national review system situated within public health; Northern Ireland and Scotland do not have CDR systems.

LEGISLATION

In many countries, states and provinces legislation sets out how CDR teams should operate. It may also determine the membership of teams and duration of tenure; what cases the team must review; the number of meetings the team should hold; the organisation to whom teams are accountable; confidentiality requirements; reporting requirements; and protection offered to team members (Hochstadt, 2006). New Zealand and England are the only countries that have national legislation specifying that review must be undertaken at local level. In Australia and Canada there is no federal legislation, but in all states and provinces that have a CDR system this is mandated in legislation at state or provincial level.

> 'The strength of NSW is its legislative base. In NSW the legislation provides us with the power to compel the provision of information so the CDR team can get any information it wishes in relation to child deaths. The flip side of that is that there is very strong governance of the confidentiality of information. The information the CDR team holds is not subject to Freedom of Information, it cannot be published except for the purposes of monitoring and reporting. If anyone wants access to it then there's a whole process through which they go. They can't obtain access anyway

> unless it's under the legislation, which really limits access to research around preventing child deaths. The other strength of the legislation is that it mandates who will be members of the team.'

There is no federal mandate to undertake CDR in the US, but thirty-seven states have mandated state CDR; seven states have no state legislation; and in seven states legislation permits but does not mandate CDR. In some US states there is a mandate to review abuse and neglect deaths only, but states can and often do review other deaths as well. Eighteen US states have no legislation for local CDR; fifteen have legislation for mandatory local CDR; and in eighteen states local CDR is permitted but not mandated. As in some US states, CDR has no legislative basis in Wales.

There appear to be both advantages and disadvantages to having CDR mandated in legislation. Some people involved in CDR are of the view that legislation is invaluable because it gives them the power to compel the information they need to conduct reviews from a wide variety of sources, including the police, health, coroner or medical examiner, child welfare services, justice and education.

> 'You've got to have a legislative mandate to do CDR.'

Certainly, as seen in Chapter 3, the CDR pilot in Wales encountered a number of problems obtaining information because information sharing was not mandatory:

> The Child Death Review pilot project encountered some difficulty in locating and accessing data. This was due to data about child deaths being held by a wide range of organisations, and reluctance by some organisations to share information due to concerns about data protection (Welsh Government, 2012).

In Wisconsin there have been similar issues around access to information because CDR is not rooted in legislation. Some US states reported, however, that they have been able to obtain data without legislation.

In some countries, states or provinces legislation enables CDR teams to follow up on progress made in response to recommendations.

For example, Hochstadt (2006) reported that Illinois' legislation provides a feedback loop enabling teams to have more clout to ensure that recommendations and action plans are implemented. Illinois' legislation mandates that recommendations made by any of the nine regional CDR teams concerning the child protective service system be sent to the director of the Department of Children and Family Services, and that the director must respond within ninety days. This feedback loop ensures that action plans are monitored and implemented. Legislation that specifies such reporting back mechanisms can be helpful, and teams that do not have mandated authority to follow up on their recommendations often reported that they struggled to ensure their recommendations were implemented.

> 'New Zealand child and youth mortality review is mandated legislatively. It gives a holistic view of the life of the child but it has no teeth to make recommendations.'

Legislation frequently includes confidentiality provisions, which can also be useful.

> 'There were strict confidentiality requirements, it was a big issue. It freed government representatives to be independent and confidentiality enabled agency representatives to be franker than they might have been otherwise. They were able to step outside of departmental constraints'.

In some places confidentiality requirements protected members of CDR teams by indemnifying them against any potential legal action arising from their work on the team. In some US states, however, people involved in CDR felt such legislation would not hold up in court; others felt there were other ways to obtain protection than through legislation.

There can be some disadvantages to having strict confidentiality provisions within legislation if this means CDR teams are not permitted to share their reports. Such provisions are useful in terms of protecting the identity of children who have died but can limit the extent to which the learning from CDR can be maximised. They can also be a source of frustration for staff and families who have been involved in child death reviews, because they may be unable to obtain feedback unless they can pursue this through Freedom of Information procedures.

> 'We are trying to think of ways of making the learning and themes more open to the key players. We can't give the reports to agencies. We can only show them an extract so they can comment on factual accuracy. We need to spread the learning.'

As a result interviewees in some places that have legislation reported that they would like to amend it because it was overly restrictive. For example, in one US state legislation capped membership of the CDR team at twelve and people involved in CDR in this state wanted to change this so they could invite additional members on to the team.

In England the legislation offers more flexibility because it states that CDOPs should have a fixed core membership but have flexibility to co-opt other relevant professionals as and when appropriate. California's legislation was written in the 1980s, and some commentators felt it was now out of date and in need of amendment.

Focus of review

There is considerable variation in the focus of review across states, provinces and countries. In particular there is a notable distinction between public health and child welfare approaches to CDR. Public health approaches involve review of every child death from every cause; child welfare approaches involve review of deaths related to abuse or neglect, or of children known to the child welfare system only.

Most countries, states and provinces have a combination of both approaches. While many places have developed processes for reviewing all child deaths, or all unexpected deaths up to age eighteen from all causes they usually continue to review abuse and neglect deaths or deaths of children known to the child welfare system through separate often internal review processes. For example, New Zealand has had a public health-focused CDR system for a decade now but still has a separate internal review process for cases in which children are known to child protective services. England and Wales have both introduced comprehensive CDR systems in the last few years yet continue to operate parallel review systems for deaths related to abuse and neglect and cases of serious injury. In contrast to processes in some other countries these review processes are multi-disciplinary in the UK and not restricted to the practice of child welfare agencies only.

In most US states the CDR function has broadened over the years. CDR processes were originally established to examine child abuse and neglect cases and tended to be located within child welfare or justice. Over time, however, the focus of review has become all deaths or all unexpected deaths, and in many states the CDR function has moved into public health and away from child welfare or justice. Despite this overall change, some states still have a mandate to review only abuse and neglect deaths, and as in other countries many states maintain separate internal review process for deaths of children known to the child welfare system. Some states do have more integrated processes: for example, in Delaware the Child Death, Near Death and Stillbirth Commission reviews all deaths but has three separate regional child death panels, one of which has responsibility for reviewing abuse and neglect deaths across the state.

In some Australian states, most notably Queensland and WA, CDR is still very focused around a child welfare model of review, and only deaths known to child protective services are reviewed. Such a model can severely limit the prevention potential of CDR, because CDR teams are able to make recommendations only to child protection agencies.

Even when all child deaths are reviewed the maximum age of review may vary. Most places review deaths up to age eighteen, but New Zealand and some parts of the US examine cases up to twenty-five. They believe this is useful because research relating to the brain development of young people has shown that brains continue to develop until age twenty-five. This may account for some of the high-risk-taking behaviour associated with deaths of young people described in the next chapter.

Some CDR teams — for example, the SA team and teams in some US states — review cases of serious injury as well as child deaths. Professionals involved in CDR, both in places that do and do not review cases of serious injury, acknowledge that there can be a lot of learning to be gleaned from cases in which children do not die. For every child who dies there are several hundred that are hospitalised as a result of injury (Stone, 2011), so being able to work within a broader injury framework that includes consideration of morbidity and mortality data broadens the evidence base.

> '... mortality is only the tip of the iceberg'.

> 'We only see deaths ... we need some sort of balance ... It's important to remember that for every suicide where a young person didn't get mental health services there are a 100 other young people receiving mental health services who don't die ... I think it would be good to look at near misses, about what actually happened to them, what actually made the difference.'

In areas where there are only a small number of deaths there can be significant issues regarding the quality of CDR data, and quality can be strengthened by analysing data from serious injuries as well as deaths. Being able to look at injuries in conjunction with deaths strengthens the public health potential of CDR considerably and can be very useful in terms of informing prevention.

> 'We've come to the point where we need to have a public health lens put on the reviews so if we looked at suicides we'd also look at all the near-miss suicides and gather that information into the review. We tried that at one point; we looked for example at a death — it was a transport death, and it was a known road where young people go and if they travel really fast they can become airborne and so two young people died at that location doing that ... The project officer looked at what other incidents had occurred at that spot and found that the coroner had an inquest into a death that were not young people but in exactly the same circumstances several years before. And there had been a number of other incidents at that particular place. And so when we made inquiries we found that in fact the local council had money to install what they call traffic calming devices at that location and so all we did there was note that this was happening, put all that information together and then check a year later that those devices had been installed and what

> the outcomes of using them had been. And so it was like you put that different kind of framework around it ... What's the easiest method of prevention? Changing the road, not restricting licences ... but you only get that perspective by working with partners or people who are involved in that kind of work and so it's putting that kind of framework around some of the deaths and incorporating that notion of working from a serious injury database as well. Whereas you may only have one death in those circumstances you might find there are lots of near misses and so putting that framework around it to make recommendations that are more broad. So I think we're confident that that kind of public health framework which incorporates serious injury will work well with those kinds of deaths where there's an obvious spine for prevention.'

Funding

CDR systems differ according to whether or not they are funded and whether or not funding is provided for dedicated review teams. When CDR was implemented in Australia, Canada, NZ, England and Wales a certain amount of dedicated funding was provided by federal or state governments. In most of these places funding has continued, but support was provided in England for only the first three years of operation, and CDOPs are unsure what will happen regarding the funding situation in the future.

CDR has been particularly well funded in Australia and Canada, where dedicated teams of professionals have been recruited to review cases full time. This contrasts with review teams in New Zealand, the US, England and Wales, where individuals have other roles and devote their time voluntarily. Some CDR teams in Australia and Canada have produced excellent thematic reports based on analysis of aggregated data partly because they have dedicated research or epidemiology support to do this. In contrast, many US teams are no longer able to produce annual reports because their funding has been withdrawn or substantially reduced in recent years.

In New Zealand the Ministry of Health played a major role in providing finance for local co-ordinators to input data into a national database. They also provided funding for a data group based at the University of Otago to analyse the data at a national level. This kind of data support is crucial. CDR can function really well only if resources are committed to useful analysis of the data.

Adequate resources have not been devoted to data analysis at a national level in England, where CDOP members report that they spend considerable time inputting information for the Department of Health but receive little useful information back.

Some CDR teams were reasonably well funded in the US when they were first established, but the level of funding for CDR as a whole is decreasing across the US and many states no longer have dedicated funding streams for undertaking reviews: for example, California used to have a state council but this has been disbanded because of budget cuts. There is a mandate to collect information on abuse and neglect deaths, and this is fulfilled by giving local CDR teams a small sum of money to input data. Similarly Washington had a statewide panel funded by public health, which enabled them to maintain a robust database of all child deaths across the state, but this has been disbanded as a result of funding cuts and only seventeen of the thirty local teams that originally existed in Washington now review cases. This means that statewide data no longer exists in Washington, which severely hampers the prevention potential of CDR across the state.

Where dedicated funding is available in the US it tends to come from the federal maternal and child health block grant, but some teams are funded through general state revenue funds. Some states have more than one funding source, and some have unusual funding structures: for example, Arizona and Nevada receive funding from death certificates; and Alabama from a tobacco settlement. Obtaining and sustaining adequate resources has been a major problem for CDR teams in the US, and budget cuts have led many teams to report that they do not have adequate resources to develop prevention programmes (Durfee *et al.*, 2002; Johnston and Covington, 2011). Although budget cuts are having a dramatic impact on CDR in the US, as will be seen in the next chapter, this has not prevented local and state teams from implementing some very successful prevention programmes. In part they have been able to do this because they have been forced to develop some very innovative partnerships with community groups and private companies precisely because they have no dedicated funds they can use for prevention.

Family involvement

There is considerable variation in the extent to which families are involved in CDR in Australia, NZ, North America and the UK. In England guidance states that families must participate, yet people included in CDR in England have reported that involving families in the rapid response process when children have only just died can be challenging. Some local teams have recruited bereavement nurses to engage with families. In Australia Victoria is the only state that includes families as a matter of course. In New Zealand families can join in but the system of participation is not particularly well developed and few families actually do take part. In Canada BC always involves families, but Ontario does not. Most US states do not include families in the review process, but families have participated in prevention campaigns, which have been developed as a result of CDR in some states: for example, in Maryland mothers whose children died in unsafe sleeping environments were involved in producing a DVD warning other mothers of the dangers.

In those states, provinces or countries where parents are included, professionals are generally supportive of this participation and report that there are mutual benefits. As was reported in previous chapters they believed that joining in can be a cathartic experience for parents and that families have a right to be involved. In some places, however, professionals distinguished between culpable and non-culpable parents and did not invite parents to participate in cases where children have been abused and neglected. Professionals also reported that family involvement is an important part of the data collection process, because families hold key information that is not known to agencies: for example, in cases of suicide professionals reported that families and friends have provided important information that has not been known previously. Some professionals stated that budgetary constraints are limiting the extent to which they can involve families. This is a particular problem in parts of Australia and Canada, where aboriginal communities in particular often live in very remote areas. CDR teams acknowledged that engaging families living in remote areas can be challenging, particularly when there are budget restrictions around the amount of travel they are able to do.

> '... here we've got the tyranny of distance — how do you properly approach a family, how do you properly hear a family if you want to meet with them when they live about 300, 400 km or further, add another zero, away'.

In some countries there are particularly sensitive issues around the involvement of aboriginal or Maori families who may be mistrustful of government agencies as a result of historical oppression. Some cultures view death and dying in a different way, and people involved in CDR need to ensure they do not offend cultural understandings of sacredness towards the dead: for example, in Maori culture post-mortems are viewed as abhorrent acts akin to desecration. This has been recognised in the Coroners Act in New Zealand, which sets out guidelines on how coroners, the police and pathologists must engage with family and community members when handling the bodies of their dead (Selket *et al.*, 2010). Some CDR team members stressed that they need to have a good understanding of these cultural issues and the importance of developing more effective ways of engaging with aboriginal communities was raised by a number of teams.

> 'Our capacity as an agency to deal with aboriginal people is a real issue for us. I mean we're a predominantly non-indigenous organisation looking at cases and deaths from a non-indigenous perspective. And we're also city dwellers but we're trying to understand the complexities of living and working in remote and regional areas.'

Some teams had recruited aboriginal staff to teach other staff about cultural issues and to help promote better relationships with aboriginal communities. In New Zealand a Maori caucus advises the national review committee. CDR teams explained that in cases where aboriginal children had died there may be a need to engage the whole community not just the child's parents.

> 'How do you engage with the broader community? Because the aboriginal communities operate as a community so who do you interview in that community? Who do you speak to?

> Because a large number of the extended family may have had some caring role with the child.'

> 'One of the things that we are doing is trying to better engage with aboriginal communities, also establishing links in different communities, in aboriginal communities, so we can call on, we can contract and employ advice ... we're really building up our knowledge of people that are out there in the field and particularly getting out into some of the aboriginal communities to get a real sense of what life's like but also to help us to better connect generally.'

In some countries or states professionals reported that families are frustrated that they are not involved.

> 'Some parents do contact us directly and often they're devastated to find that we can't either release information we have on their case or give them any background or tell them what we've written in the report or what the deliberation was.'

Some CDR teams believed that family participation is inappropriate, but in some areas CDR teams are beginning to rethink their policy around non-involvement. For example, in one Australian state after careful consideration of the merits of family involvement the CDR team decided to base their decision on whether or not to involve the family on consideration of the circumstances of each individual case.

> 'Leading up to the proclamation or the jurisdiction becoming operational we thought we must tell the family, if we're looking into the life of their deceased child we must tell them, they have a right to know. And then you get into the situation of well how much do they need to know really about what we're doing and will that cause them more stress than the benefit to the family itself? So we've determined pretty much that if a serious case occurs and we are going to go into a full investigation that we will advise the family but we'll be looking at whether that's in the best interests of the child, the other children involved and considering what other issues there are before we actually determine on how we approach that. So

> far it hasn't come up ... but we decided ... that unless we find some issues and unless we can be absolutely sure the family can contribute to our understanding we're not going to tell the family. If the family contacts us and wants to know we most certainly will talk to them and we'll tell them about the stages of our process and we'll tell them the outcome of our process, but for most cases they might identify some minor issues and it's pretty clear we don't need to ask anybody what those issues are.'

Other CDR teams have begun to acknowledge that there might be a need to speak to family members or other members of the community, but reported that they have not yet developed effective ways of doing this.

> '... because they were so important to the life of the child and the safety of the child and we would need to understand their perspective on the services and the decisions that were made and their role, and we need to understand that in order to properly determine what recommendations we need to make. But as yet we haven't got to that point and it is probably something that we'll determine as to whether it's in the families' interests for us to investigate the case. We don't want to create unnecessary fear or unnecessary grief.'

Data

A standardised data input process and standardised definitions are crucial for effective CDR.

> ... teams must make a commitment to systematically collect and report information gained from the team reviews. This requires an allocation of resources (often in-kind staff time) from one or more agencies to ensure data is collected and entered into a database and used in later analyses. Although important prevention efforts can move forward without such data (e.g. on the strength of a single case or an individual champion), the power of the CDR process for prevention lies in its ability to provide a systematic source of information on the underlying patterns of circumstances (i.e. risk

> and protective factors) surrounding child deaths (Covington and Wirtz, forthcoming).

Local teams need to collect systematically and report on information gained from reviews, and many countries, states or provinces provide training, technical assistance and support for this. There also needs to be consistency and standardisation and aggregation of data at a national level, so that major issues and trends in child mortality can be identified and evidence-based national prevention initiatives implemented. Variation in the way in which CDR is undertaken across states and provinces in Australia and Canada means it is not possible to obtain reliable national data in these countries. Nevertheless because CDR has been well resourced in these countries many states and provinces in Australia and Canada have very good-quality, state-level data that has enabled them to undertake excellent aggregate or cohort reviews that have effectively informed policy and practice and led to effective prevention initiatives. Some of these will be discussed in the next chapter.

CDR is also organised in different ways across the US. Thirty-six states now use the MCHB-funded US NCCDR case reporting system, so there is some degree of consistency in terms of data collection, and information on more than 88,000 deaths is now held in a national database. There are, however, limitations to this national data. The NCCDR has done an incredible job in ensuring that basic demographic questions are covered in reviews across a large number of states, but Covington (2011) conceded that the data is limited. Most importantly, it cannot be compared state to state, and sometimes even team to team within a state, because of variation in the types and timing of reviews. There are also differences in the quality of data between teams and states. Some of the data elements are subjective and can be interpreted differently by different teams: for example, whether the death was preventable and whether an act of omission contributed to the death. Some individuals involved in CDR warned that it may actually be futile spending too much time looking at whether an individual death is or is not preventable.

> 'It doesn't matter if that death was preventable or not it's what can we learn from that death that would allow us to

influence the well-being of other children in the community. I'm less clear why people focus on that because it's irrelevant for the kids who died and it's irrelevant for future prevention ... We spent a lot of time and energy on that and it didn't really change anything.'

There are lessons here for England, where national government determined that local teams should decide how many deaths are preventable and report this figure back to the government.

There is also some missing data in the national database in the US because teams do not always answer some of the harder questions or the right people are not coming to CDR meetings so not all of the questions can be answered. Lastly there can be a significant time lag between a child dying, a review being undertaken and data being entered into the database (Covington, 2011).

New Zealand's national co-ordinated system whereby all local health boards input data into a national database was based on the US model. There is now ten years of in-depth data on every child who has died in New Zealand, and this can be used to inform national policy and practice around prevention. As in the US there are some issues around definitions, but the system has been well resourced and the research potential of the data is enormous.

In England LSCBs provide an annual return to the Department for Education, but the amount and quality of comparable information is not as good as in New Zealand, because there has been less commitment to undertake useful analysis of the national data. Wales also has a national database of information on every child who has died since 2008 and is beginning to build up enough cases to be able to undertake meaningful analysis at a national level.

CONCLUSION

- CDR is rooted in legislation in most countries, but it is not mandated in Wales or in all US states. There are advantages and disadvantages associated with legislation.
- There is a notable difference between public health and child welfare approaches to CDR. Most countries adopt both

approaches in tandem, but some places — for example, some Australian states — lean towards a child-welfare approach.

- In some places CDR teams are able to review cases of serious injury as well as the deaths of all children from all causes. This is more congruent with a public health approach and may offer the most learning in terms of prevention.
- Some places have made significant efforts to involve families and communities in CDR and believe this to be worthwhile, but most countries still do not routinely involve families in CDR.
- New Zealand and England are the only countries to have national co-ordinated systems, where all deaths are reviewed at local level and information is inputted at local level but aggregated data is also available at national level. Wales has a national database of all deaths but does not review all deaths. Review processes vary considerably across states and provinces in Australia, the US and Canada. No national data exists in Australia or Canada. Thirty-six states in the US use a national case recording system, so some limited national data is available.

CHAPTER 5

Key themes and prevention initiatives

Introduction

> 'It's the tangible things you can do that seem to make the difference so concentrate efforts on bicycle helmets for children to prevent head injury ... and safe cribs supplying a safe place for a baby to sleep. That's very tangible — it's something you can literally get your hands on and do.'

> A key function of CDR is to develop preventative actions that will protect children. It has a unique capacity to provide an ecological understanding of child mortality and catalyse evidence-based, multi-level prevention strategies (Desapriya *et al.*, 2011).

> 'We have a broader perspective on a young person's life than the coroner does.'

> 'It's about finding things that work and penetrating all systems and changing them.'

The main reasons why children die are remarkably consistent across Australia, New Zealand, the US, Canada, England and Wales. CDR teams in all these countries are identifying and grappling with the same kinds of themes such as unsafe sleeping, lack of parental supervision, and risk-taking behaviour among adolescents. Many CDR teams across these countries group reviews by cause of death, so they can focus recommendations around particular themes and target prevention activity at reducing specific types of deaths. This chapter considers the key themes and issues that have been identified across Australia, New Zealand, North America and the UK, and it outlines some of the prevention strategies that have been implemented at local, state and national level in an attempt to tackle some of these issues.

TYPES OF PREVENTION

CDR can lead to different kinds of prevention activity. Hochstadt (2006) outlined that action plans and recommendations of CDR teams fall into three broad categories:

- *Case specific:* recommendations that require action on a specific case. For example, following the death of a child, protective services may be directed to obtain medical examinations of surviving siblings or provide grief counselling for family members.
- *Systemic:* recommendations requiring actions that have broader implications for the many systems that impinge on the safety and well-being of children. For example, Hochstadt reported that the Cook County, Illinois, CDR team recommended that the state protective service agency develops specific guidelines for the number of children who can reside in foster homes as a function of the acuity of care required by the children in residence. Many of the recommendations in SCR reports in the UK are systemic recommendations.
- *Prevention and public health:* action plans outlining primary prevention efforts, which may involve changes in public policy and legislation. For example, Hochstadt (2006) reported that Iowa's CDR team recommended that the Community Empowerment Initiative be expanded throughout Iowa to provide home visits for all families with newborn children.

Successful prevention campaigns usually involve more than one type of activity: for example, campaigns to reduce the number of children and young people dying in motor vehicle accidents may include changes to road design, new legislation, promotion of car seats, as well as education in schools and local communities. CDR teams, therefore, need to partner with a wide range of agencies, some of whom may not be represented on CDR teams, in order to fulfil the prevention part of their remit. This can prove challenging.

Types of prevention initiatives

- *Environmental modification*: for example, in BC the CDR team worked with transport agencies to modify a bridge after several young people died from jumping off it.

- *Produce modification*: for example, the CDR team worked with drug companies to ensure that child safety tops were placed on methadone bottles; CDOPs in the West Midlands in England worked with window blind manufacturers after a number of children died after being caught in window or door cords.
- *Legislation, regulation and enforcement*: for example, the work of CDR teams in NZ and Australia led to legislation around pool fencing to reducing drowning deaths.
- *Promoting the use of safety devices such as smoke detectors, seat belts and car seats*: for example, implementation of local bike helmet ordinances in Washington.
- *Supportive home visits to families of young children*: for example, the home-visiting scheme in Sacramento, California, which was targeted at high-risk families was a recommendation of the CDR team.
- *Education such as school-based programmes or media work in the community to promote knowledge*: for example, public service announcements on local Delaware Valley radio stations in relation to safe sleeping; campaigns to promote safe storage of firearms in Washington.

Moving from recommendations to prevention

This can be difficult, not least because of the number of partners that need to be involved. As we have seen many CDR teams do not have adequate resources to conduct public health campaigns in support of prevention objectives and/or have no mandate to do this kind of work (Johnston and Covington, 2011). Because they have no budget to develop new initiatives some CDR teams have put enormous efforts into strengthening existing programmes in their community: for example, following a review of suicide cases the King County team in Washington wanted to try and reduce the number of teen suicides but had no budget to develop new programmes. There was, however, already a grant in place to provide suicide prevention training in schools and community agencies in the county. The CDR team, therefore, recommended that a letter be signed by the Director of Public Health recommending this training be undertaken by anyone working with young people. The CDR team in Outagamie in Wisconsin similarly ensured that their youth suicide strategy built on existing systems and capacity within the community.

CDR activity is routinely included in public health press releases in Washington: for example, at the onset of the swimming season there is always a press release about drowning, which includes information from CDR. Professionals involved in CDR in Washington feel, however, that such messages do not always get to the right people. Some felt it would be useful to have a media person on CDR teams to get the messages out effectively in the community.

> 'The problem with public health doing the press releases is it doesn't always hit the families who need to hear the message … there isn't a way of getting that sort of information out.'

The Sacramento local team use CDR information to drive funding proposals and have had some success with this.

> 'We say this clearly seems like a need based on the number of children who are dying and the risk factors associated with it and so we'll apply for grants for that.'

In order to be effective CDR recommendations should be grounded in the best available evidence. CDR teams, therefore, needed to review the research literature and recognise prevention sites to find interventions that have been successful elsewhere (Covington and Wirtz, forthcoming). Washington used to have a best practices website that gave local teams across the state a framework they could use for implementing prevention strategies. This ensured that messaging was consistent across local teams: for example, a purple crying programme was implemented across the state following an increase in deaths and injuries from abusive head trauma, because evidence from a large study in North Carolina demonstrated it could result in positive changes in behaviour.

New Zealand's traffic light test

New Zealand is a small country with a population of just 4.5 million, and professionals involved in CDR there recognise that they need to look further afield for evidence of good practice in other countries. The national review group in New Zealand carry out systematic reviews of the literature at the Cochrane level to put their national recommendations into perspective and to find out whether they are supported by what the literature suggests is promising practice. A group of advisers who are experts in their field, for example, representatives from Safekids, from the Office of the Children's Commissioner and experts in road safety and water safety are represented on the national team. The advisers provide examples of best practice from their area of expertise and advise on and test all of the national recommendations using a 'traffic light test':

- a green light is awarded when there is strong evidence to suggest that an initiative works and is a good idea;
- a red light is given when the international evidence base suggests that the initiative may be counter-productive or will make no difference;
- an amber light suggests the initiative may potentially be a good idea but that more needs to be found out about it.

This approach was used to develop initiatives to prevent the deaths of young drivers. International evidence has shown that zero tolerance on alcohol for young drivers works, so the national group in New Zealand recommended the introduction of a zero tolerance policy in their own country as a way of reducing the number of motor vehicle deaths involving young people.

Developing recommendations in BC

In preparation for recommendation development the CDR unit in BC identify best and most promising prevention practices by reviewing research literature and exploring interventions that have shown success in other jurisdictions. Stakeholder consultations are also conducted to ensure recommendations are informed by the knowledge of people in the field. The US NCCDR have a recommendation development tool that the CDR unit use to ensure recommendations are evidence based, feasible and linked to their case review findings. Recommendations are also considered in the context of the spectrum of prevention to ensure the proposed actions reflect a multi-faceted approach.

TYPES OF DEATH AND PREVENTION INITIATIVES

Deaths from natural causes

The largest proportion of deaths, around half of all deaths, across the six countries are from natural causes but not all of these deaths will be expected. Many CDR teams believed it was important to review natural deaths as well as unnatural deaths, because even if the death is caused by an underlying medical cause review can still identify modifiable risk factors, particularly when deaths are unexpected.

For example, a child may have had limited access to paediatric care, and it is possible that their life may have been saved if they had been able to receive medical care more promptly. This can be a particular risk factor for children living in rural or remote areas. For most CDR teams, however, the primary focus of review is what we can learn from unexpected deaths from non-natural causes.

Sudden unexpected infant deaths

The second highest category of deaths overall and the highest proportion of unexpected deaths are sudden infant deaths (SIDs) and Sudden Unexpected Infant Deaths (SUIDs) or Sudden Unexpected Deaths in Infants (SUDIs). SIDs is not a cause of death but a medical term indicating the exclusion of other factors. SIDs are a type of SUID/SUDI. Definitions of SIDs and SUIDs/SUDIs may vary considerably across and even within the same country or state depending on who the coroner is, and CDR can be a useful way of checking out coroner's determinations and identifying misclassification of infant deaths.

- SIDs is 'the sudden death of an infant, which is unexplained after the review of the clinical history, examination of the circumstances of death and post-mortem examination' (Rognum and Willinger, 1995).
- SUIDs/SUDIs encompasses SIDs deaths as well as more grey scenarios: deaths in the presence of known risk factors such as cigarette smoke, prematurity, bed sharing or minor infections where the contribution of the risk factor remains uncertain (Fleming *et al.*, 2006).

The number of SIDs deaths across Australia, New Zealand, North America and the UK have levelled off in recent years following a substantial drop in the 1990s, which resulted from campaigns to ensure babies slept on their backs in an attempt to reduce the number of 'cot deaths'.

Data from CDR has been useful in informing our knowledge of infant deaths. Most SUIDs are of previously healthy infants. A high proportion of these deaths may be preventable, but information on death certificates can be very limited in relation to the context of the death. The mechanism of death on death certificates is often unknown, especially in relation to whether bed sharing or co-sleeping was a factor. CDR data provides far richer contextual information that has enabled us to determine potential risk factors for SUDI/SUIDs. CDR has demonstrated that infants sleep in unsafe situations for a number of reasons including lack of awareness, the infant being unsettled, lack of a cot, household overcrowding or the house being too cold. In some instances infants normally sleep in a safe place but may sleep in an unsafe arrangement because of a social gathering or because one or more of their parents or caregivers is intoxicated.

A number of CDR teams have identified that a disproportionate number of black and ethnic minority (BME) children are dying in unsafe sleeping environments. For example, in Delaware the Child Death Panel reviewed eighteen deaths related to unsafe infant sleeping practices, and in twelve of these cases — 67% — the child was an African–American infant.

SUDI RISK FACTORS

- being male;
- fetal exposure to cigarette smoke;
- postnatal exposure to cigarette smoke;
- recent viral illness;
- aboriginal ancestry;
- being placed in a non-supine position;
- a cluttered sleep environment;
- bed sharing;
- overheating;
- sleeping on a soft surface not intended for infant sleep;
- parental substance use;
- poverty;
- low maternal and educational age;
- inadequate prenatal care.

CDR teams across Australia, New Zealand, North America and the UK all report that they are reviewing high numbers of deaths of babies in unsafe sleep environments. A high proportion of these deaths may be preventable, and all teams are focusing efforts on preventing these types of death.

> 'As much effort needs to be put into ensuring infants have a safe place to sleep as is currently put into having a safe place to ride in cars.'

In Wisconsin one small community provided community education around safe sleep after reviewing eight deaths in a two-year period. They wanted to give professionals — for example, probation and parole and child protection professionals — the right words to use to start a conversation with parents without sounding judgemental. They built in an evaluation component to find out whether professionals had learned anything. They also purchased cribs for families. When a crib was given to a family they were provided with information about safe sleeping, and feedback was obtained in relation to how they used the crib.

US SUID case registry

The US SUID case registry pilot project is an excellent example of how CDR data can be used at a national level to improve our understanding of why children die and enable us to develop evidence-based initiatives to try to prevent deaths.

The project is funded by the US Centers for Disease Control and Prevention (CDC) and is being piloted in seven states: Colorado, Georgia, Michigan, New Jersey, New Mexico, Minnesota and New Hampshire. The aim of the project is to prevent infant deaths to:

- ❑ provide more comprehensive data to enable better identification of SUID cases;
- ❑ determine which factors in the sleep environment contribute to SUID cases to enable better identification of high risk groups in order to target interventions.

The SUID case registry is a state population based surveillance system that builds on CDR data. It is 'a vehicle for driving data to action'. SUID-specific variables around the sleep environment have been added to the data that is normally recorded by CDR teams using the national case reporting system to establish what was going on in the child's environment at the time of death. For example, there are questions about mothers' pregnancies and whether they smoked; there are also infant health questions relating to the seventy-two hours before death, such as whether children were sick or had had immunisations. A number of systems variables have also been added. Data collection begins at the death scene, so death scene investigation and recording, including witness statements, are being improved and scene re-enactments undertaken. CDR teams are also being given increased access to autopsy information. Improved national reporting will enable better identification of SUIDs, determine which factors in the sleep environment contribute to SUIDs and enable better identification of high risk groups to inform interventions, affect policy and practise change and prevent deaths.

Early evidence suggests that the SUID pilot process is leading to improvements in the quality of all child death reviews – not just SUID cases. One CDR expert suggested that there should be a similar pilot focusing on abuse and neglect deaths, since only CDR teams can count such deaths accurately.

Infant safe sleeping initiatives, Delaware

In Delaware the Infant Safe Sleeping Practice Subcommittee was created after the CDNDSC reviewed fifty-seven infant and child sleep-related deaths in 2003–7. The subcommittee, a community action team, aimed to address this significant problem and embarked on a media campaign to increase awareness of safe sleeping practices. The campaign included exterior and interior prevention messages on buses throughout the state and public service announcements on local radio stations. The campaign was funded by a grant from the Delaware SIDs Affiliate. The strong visual images from the campaign were used to develop posters and billboards with the same images. Through collaboration with the Delaware Healthy Mother Infant Consortium and the Division of Public Health, 4,000 posters were developed in English and Spanish and distributed to licensed day-care centres throughout the state.

The CDNDSC believed that prevention efforts also needed to be disseminated at a local, grassroots level. They participated in seven community events promoting safe sleeping practices for infants. They also developed a training programme for professionals, presenting the same training session throughout the state to physicians, nurses, social workers and day-care workers. Training was taken to professionals at their place of work. Training locations included a day-care centre that had experienced a child death as a result of unsafe sleeping practices.

In June 2009 a partnership was developed between the Delaware Division of Public Health, Nemours Health and Prevention Services of the Nemours Foundation (Nemours) and the CDNDSC to implement the first Cribs for Kids (www.CribsforKids.org) programme in Delaware. Research has shown that babies who sleep in unsafe sleep environments, including adult beds, are at a forty times greater risk of dying. Cribs for Kids is a safe-sleep evidence-based education programme to help reduce the risk of injury and death of infants due to unsafe sleep environments. It has had very good outcomes in other states in reducing infant unsafe sleeping deaths. A Graco Pack 'n' Play crib and educational materials regarding safe sleeping and other important safety tips were given to parents. Any mother was entitled to a free crib if she met the following criteria:

- was unable to purchase a crib by any other means;
- was due to deliver the baby in six weeks;

- had an infant who is younger than six months of age.

In Delaware the education on unsafe sleeping practices for infants was provided to the family by a Division of Public Health nurse. Delaware is the only state to offer this education in the home, and has been recognised by national leaders as the gold standard in comparison with other states, where the family have to pick up a crib from an office or facility. Among the 120 cribs that were delivered in 2010 through the Delaware Cribs for Kids programme, no deaths occurred in those families because of unsafe infant sleeping.

The CDNDSC also partnered with A.I. duPont Hospital for Children to implement mandatory education for nursing staff on infant safe-sleeping practices and with the Delaware Ecumenical Council to develop a brochure on infant safe-sleeping practices for clergy and others to utilise within their faith community.

Unexpected injury deaths

If natural deaths and SIDs/SUIDs are removed, the remaining deaths are unexpected injury deaths, which can be split between:

- *unintentional injury*: road traffic deaths; drowning deaths; deaths from fire or poisoning;
- *intentional injury*: deaths from suicide; self-harm; interpersonal violence (homicide, child abuse and neglect).

A high proportion of unintentional injury deaths among young people may be caused by risk-taking behaviour — voluntary behaviours associated with a heightened risk of injury or death, such as reckless use of alcohol or other substances, or reckless driving. Across all six countries more boys die from unintentional injuries than girls. Boys are most likely to be at higher risk because they have a greater propensity for risk-taking behaviour or exposure to hazardous environments.

The highest proportion of unintentional injury deaths in all six countries are from transport-related events, predominantly motor vehicle crashes. There are also a number of pedestrian deaths caused by a motor vehicle, which include a small number of driveway run-over deaths, as well as a number of cycle deaths. In New Zealand young people comprise 14% of the total population but almost 33% of all motor vehicle crash deaths. Mortality rates for males in transport-related events are more than twice the rate for females, and the Maori rate is more than double that of non-Maori (CYMRC, 2009). Young drivers are particularly at risk, and CDR in NZ has demonstrated that the greatest risk period for young drivers is in the first six months of driving.

CDR has enabled the identification of common conditions associated with transport-related mortality. These include night driving, high speeds, poor visibility, weather, alcohol and drug use, driving on rural roads and drivers being distracted by cell phone use. There is clear evidence of a geographical influence in relation to motor-vehicle-related deaths. There are more serious accidents on rural roads, and rural areas, therefore, tend to have higher rates of mortality from motor vehicle accidents than urban areas. Different patterns of death in rural and urban areas lend support to the argument that CDR works best as a local process, where prevention activity can be better targeted towards local needs and the peculiarities of local environments.

Some people involved in CDR reported that accidents were almost expected in rural areas and that we needed to change this mindset. While it may be useful to have local teams that can respond to local need it is also invaluable for teams to interact and share good practice with other teams who may be experiencing similar cases. Some areas experience the same sorts of deaths over and over: for example, in Detroit there have been a lot of gunshot deaths of teenagers with no known perpetrator, and it can be difficult for teams to continue to come up with recommendations to target these kinds of deaths when they see little evidence that numbers are reducing. In these kinds of situations CDR team members acknowledge that it can be good to share experiences with teams in other areas: for example, other cities such as Atlanta have a similar profile of deaths and have faced similar challenges.

Alcohol has been shown to have a greater effect on driving performance at lower levels for young people compared to older age groups, and studies in the US that have introduced zero blood alcohol content for young people have shown a significant reduction in fatal crashes involving single vehicles at night. In New Zealand the national CYMRC now supports zero blood alcohol content for young and novice drivers.

Many CDR teams have introduced prevention initiatives to try to reduce motor vehicle related deaths.

- In Colorado CDR review findings have motivated prevention activities such as the development of child passenger safety seat promotion programmes, increase in seat belt usage and awareness, and creation of graduated licensing law restrictions.
- A statewide graduated driver's licence was introduced in Washington in the 1990s as a result of a recommendation made following review of aggregated child death data.
- In Georgia many local community changes have occurred as a result of CDR recommendations including new traffic lights and a crosswalk connecting two busy malls.
- In BC the CDRU systematically collects data on adult supervision among fatal childhood injuries. Results of a review of child pedestrian fatalities showed that only a third of children below ten years of age were under active supervision of an adult at the time of the fatal incident (Desapriya *et al.*, 2011). This finding supported the need to raise awareness of child pedestrian injury and improve supervision practices among parents and caregivers.

Adolescents also die from poisoning from alcohol or drugs and from drowning. Alcohol contributes to motor vehicle deaths, suicide, poisoning and drowning and stricter controls on alcohol may impact on all such categories of death. Increased risk of drowning after age thirteen seems to reflect increasing exposure to risky situations, less supervision and poor perception of risk together with the influence of drugs and alcohol (McDonald *et al.*, 2005).

Preschool age children are also at greater risk of drowning. Males are more likely to die from drowning across countries, and in New Zealand the Maori rate is 2.1 times higher than the non-Maori rate (CYMRC, 2010). Some areas have unusual patterns in relation to drowning deaths: for example, Alaska has a higher than average rate of drowning deaths, and CDR has revealed that a number of these deaths are related to snow machine accidents where children have fallen through the ice. This is another example of the benefit of having a local review process.

CDR data has identified that most drowning deaths of younger children are related to lack of adult supervision in a pool or bathtub, whereas adolescents tend to drown in rivers or in the sea. Parents may leave children in the bath to see to other children or to do household tasks. Sometimes they leave them in the care of siblings, who may not be suitable caregivers. Some infants are left in bath seats and fall out. Bath seats can give parents a false sense of security, and the European child safety alliance now recommends they should not be used. Deaths in baths also occur in older age groups, where children have medical conditions such as epilepsy.

RISK FACTORS FOR DROWNING

- lack of adult supervision;
- risk-taking behaviour.

The Delaware CDR Commission reviewed seven deaths from drowning between 2008 and 2009. Three of the deaths were in a pool, one was in a hot tub and three were in a bathtub. The dominant theme throughout the deaths was that the child was not supervised.

Drowning deaths of children of all ages are largely preventable if adequate supervision and appropriate environmental safeguards are in place, so many CDR teams have implemented prevention initiatives to try to reduce the number of such deaths. For example:

- Colorado initiated a public awareness campaign on bucket drowning prevention.
- In Washington CDR data was used to document the disproportionate risk of drowning among Asian immigrant youth, in open water and at unguarded public parks. The data was used to inform policy development and carefully focused drowning prevention campaigns (Quan *et al.*, 2011). A law has now been passed in Washington that if you swim at a lake or river in the county you have to wear a flotation device.

Across the six countries suicide accounts for a varying proportion of the deaths of young people from aged ten. Males are more likely to die from suicide in all countries. They are not, however, necessarily more likely to attempt suicide; rather they tend to use more lethal means. In New Zealand Maori rates are more than two times higher than non-Maori rates (CYMRC, 2010). In Australia and Canada aboriginal rates are also substantially higher. A number of people engaged in CDR across several countries reported a worrying increase in suicides at younger ages, particularly an increase in the number of thirteen year olds.

> 'It used to be rare to see thirteen and fourteen year olds, but this is becoming common now ... Kids are more mature now — there are more things going on in their lives.'

In New Zealand and the US a choking game was cited as having resulted in a number of asphyxiation deaths of younger adolescents.

RISK FACTORS FOR SUICIDE

- mental health disorders, including depression;
- adverse experiences, including sexual, physical and emotional abuse, neglect, family breakdown, family violence;
- parental mental illness;
- alcohol and drug abuse;
- having a friend or family member attempt suicide;
- access to lethal means.

In Australia, New Zealand, Canada and the UK hanging is the most common form of suicide, while the US has a far higher number of suicides from gunshot wounds, presumably because it is easier to obtain firearms in the US than in other countries. The US also has a higher number of homicides from firearms than other countries and a higher number of accidental deaths from firearms: for example, cases where children have been killed after getting hold of a parent's gun. Many CDR teams in the US reported that it was extremely difficult to implement changes to legislation around the possession of firearms because gun ownership was deemed to be a constitutional right.

Prevention of youth and adolescent suicide in Outagamie County, Wisconsin

The Outagamie County CDR team reviewed five teen suicide deaths over a five-year period. It identified a number of risk factors based on these cases, which correlated with national evidence:

- ❑ **individual factors:** depression and other mental illness; previous suicide attempt; alcohol and/or substance abuse; and the impulsive characteristic of young people;

- **family and interpersonal factors:** childhood maltreatment; parental separation or divorce; interpersonal conflicts or losses; lack of support; suicide or suicide attempt by a relative or close friend;
- **environmental factors:** access to firearms and other lethal means; bullying; and issues of sexuality and gender identification.

In May 2010 community agencies and advocacy groups joined together to explore prevention strategies. Recommendations built on existing systems and capacity within the community and were based on identification of gaps and a review of best practices:

- increase awareness of existing mental health services among professionals and young people and the community (through posters, magnets, presentations and outreach activity);
- utilise social media and other technology of young people to promote mental health resources;
- support and sustain Question, Persuade, Refer (QPR); train-the-trainer training as a component of a community-based suicide prevention programme (700 professionals and community members trained);
- support and sustain community initiatives, mental health collaborations and coalitions for the purposes of: improving access to mental health services for children and youth; improving co-ordination and collaboration between providers; decreasing stigma; and preventing suicide;
- decrease youth access to lethal means, specifically firearms, alcohol and pharmaceuticals;
- support and sustain community initiatives, collaborations and coalitions for the purpose of increasing recognition, respect and support for lesbian, gay, bisexual and transgender (LGBT) people and creating safe spaces;
- create a community where all people are welcome, safe and valued (training in cultural competence and diversity, education and media coverage of events that bring people together).

In some countries it was reported that suicide deaths may often be recorded as undetermined deaths or deaths from misadventure. Suicide deaths may be under-reported for cultural or religious reasons or because coroners do not want to upset families because of the stigma associated with suicide.

> 'All coroners are closed shops and shouldn't be so. The CDR team being able to call into question what the coroner's doing is a very important thing … Coroners and forensic pathologists take certain decisions based on what they

> think parents might want to hear, so you know it's too painful so let's just avoid it, but it's not — the parents want to know what happened.'

This variable classification may partially explain why some countries — for example, New Zealand — appear to have a high suicide rate compared to other countries. NZ has the highest rates of youth suicide in the Organisation for Economic Co-operation and Development (OECD) (CYMRC, 2010), but rates across countries are not comparable because the level of proof required for classification for suicide varies considerably. NZ has a low number of undetermined deaths compared to other countries, suggesting that coroners in NZ may be less likely than coroners in other countries to classify suicide deaths as undetermined. There can be conflict between coroners' records and CDR data in relation to suicide, and CDR can be a useful way of highlighting these kinds of issues around classification.

> 'We don't have to take what the coroner says so that's the beauty of our committee. We're completely independent so the committee can decide, can make a ruling, even if it's in complete contrast to what the coroner says, and we do that not infrequently, not frequently but it does happen.'

In some cases of suicide it is not always easy to determine whether injury was intentional or not, and CDR teams may be better placed to determine this than coroners.

> 'In some circumstances we've been less than happy about the coronial conclusion on a case, which may be to protect the family, where there have been certainly implications from the information we've had that there may well have been intent.'

Across Australia, NZ, North America and the UK only very small numbers of children and young people die from intentional injury at the hands of others. A very small number of infants and young children die from homicide, usually at the hands of their parents. Some of these infants die from head injuries as a result of shaken baby syndrome, and a number of CDR teams have enacted prevention activities around this. A small number of teenagers also die from homicide, but teenagers are more likely to be killed by their peers than their parents.

Abusive Head Trauma Program, Delaware

The CDNDSC's review of thirteen deaths and near deaths involving abusive head trauma in Delaware demonstrated the need for preventive parent education on abusive head trauma. The CDNDSC partnered with Prevent Child Abuse Delaware to introduce a comprehensive statewide parent education Abusive Head Trauma Program. After review of nationwide parent education programmes, they selected an evidence-based model from Pennsylvania, which when replicated in other states demonstrated a reduction in the number of infant abusive head trauma cases. The Delaware programme was financed by a grant from AstraZeneca and Barclaycard US. A nurse educator trains all nursing staff in birthing hospitals across the state. After training, the hospital nursing staff show each mother and father or caregiver a ten-minute DVD before they are discharged from hospital. The DVD shows three families who have experienced the tragedy of abusive head trauma. The possible injuries from shaking are identified as well as the outcome of the three families. After watching the DVD parents sign a consent form stating that they watched the DVD and understand its content. If they choose to they can provide their phone number to receive a follow-up phone call, which is made by a social worker, six to seven weeks after the baby is born. If the parent needs additional support at the time of the phone call, appropriate referrals and resources will be provided. This six/seven-week period has been shown to be the peak of an infant's crying and, therefore, the period of greatest risk for abusive head trauma. If a child has been abused after education on abusive head trauma, this will be reflected through medical record abstraction at the Child Abuse and Neglect Panel.

Despite the small numbers of children dying from homicide and abuse and neglect-related deaths data from CDR teams has motivated prevention activities to tackle such deaths in a number of areas. Laws on child homicide sentencing, safely surrendered babies, children left alone in cars (Kaitlyn's Law) and zero tolerance for carrying guns on school property have all been enacted as a result of CDR (Hochstadt, 2006). In Alabama the CDR team identified a number of newborn infants who had been abandoned or left to die. They partnered with local media and developed a programme called 'Safe Place', which allowed mothers to leave newborns who were less than seventy-two hours old at hospital emergency departments with no questions asked. This model has now been replicated across many other US states (Wirtz *et al.*, 2011). California's CDR findings have motivated prevention activities including public education on child maltreatment prevention in general, and more specifically in relation to shaken baby prevention, perinatal substance exposure and parental substance abuse. In Georgia statewide changes have occurred in child protection policy as a result of recommendations from CDR: all child abuse and neglect reports of children less than one now require a fully undressed examination by a professional.

Even single cases in which children have died from abuse and neglect may result in significant prevention activity. For example, in a local community in Washington a case of a six-week-old baby who died from head injuries resulted in a change in practice across the area. It was found that the child's mother had taken the baby to her doctor, and the baby had facial bruising, but the doctor had failed to report this because the bruising could have been inflicted by other children in the household. The CDR team made a recommendation to the CA that since non-mobile babies should not present with bruises all cases where babies presented with bruises should be screened for investigation. The department accepted the recommendation, and this has now become standard procedure.

Tackling medical neglect deaths in Sacramento County, California

A couple of years ago the Sacramento County CDR team examined several child abuse and neglect (CAN) homicides and found that a number of these children were medically fragile – i.e. they had some chronic health problems. In some cases they were dying because their caregivers were not taking the necessary medical precautions or not following up after treatment. They recommended that child protective services look at this issue in more depth, and they were able to identify that not only had these children died from medical neglect but they had also been receiving in-home supportive services (financial support for caregivers to look after a medically fragile child). The CDR team researched this further and found that about 65% of the children in home support services were also open to child protective services. That connection had never been made before. As a result of this research any child that is now referred to CPS that has medical issues will have a subsequent review by a new medical team.

> **'Social workers are trained to identify abuse and neglect in generally healthy children but they do not have a medical background**

— they are not nurses and doctors — and so this team suggested that nurses or doctors or a medical team do a joint visit or set up some kind of review of the case. Then they did a cross-check. All cases that had in-home supportive services were reviewed if they were an open CPS case ... the really compelling tangible result was the creation of a policy and practice change within the county that, one, saved children's lives and, two, saved money and allowed the programmes to run more efficiently.'

Child abuse identification and reporting guidelines for medical providers, Delaware

In 2009 the training programme 'Child abuse identification and reporting guidelines for medical providers' was launched in Delaware. This training was developed as a direct result of eleven cases of death and near death in which medical providers saw the child with injuries prior to the death or near death and failed to diagnose and/or report child abuse and neglect. The inaugural training was co-presented by a local physician and a division of Family Services staff member at Kent General Hospital to doctors, nurses and social workers. The CDNDSC then received a small grant to facilitate ongoing training throughout the state, and 102 medical professionals and staff had been trained by the end of 2010. Further courses were taken in 2011. Recent legislation increased the training need for the child abuse identification and reporting guidelines for Delaware medical providers to be run statewide. The legislation clarified that the mandatory duty to report child abuse or neglect applies to all persons, as well as agencies, organisations and entities.The potential civil penalties were increased for persons or entities who failed to report, with the added provision that the Department of Justice would be notified of any violations.

FACTORS ASSOCIATED WITH INCREASED RISK

There are two periods when children are at most risk of dying: in the first five years of their lives; and during adolescence. At these times peaks in mortality coincide with periods of rapid transition in the life course. Children are least likely to die during the middle years of childhood, but after the relative safety of these years rates of death increase dramatically from age fourteen, particularly for males. In adolescence a far higher proportion of fatalities are due to injury than at younger ages, and a high proportion of teenage deaths are, therefore, potentially preventable. The chair of the New Zealand national review committee has recommended that more prevention activity should be concentrated on the middle years with the aim of reducing deaths in adolescence.

BME children are significantly over-represented in CDR data: for example, Afro–American children have twice the rate of deaths of white children in Sacramento county, California, for natural and non-natural deaths, and this figure has remained consistent for more than twenty years. BME children are particularly over-represented if we consider deaths of children known to the child protection system: for example, in NSW aboriginal children constitute 25% of deaths known to the child protection system but only 4% of the population; in Victoria 12% of deaths of children known to child protection are of aboriginal children but they make up only 1% of the Victorian population.

Poverty is also a risk factor for child death. Fire-related injury deaths — a highly preventable cause of mortality — are highly correlated with deprivation. There is also an increased pedestrian casualty risk to children from poorer backgrounds, possibly because of less adult supervision or more risky behavioural patterns. Poverty has also been recognised as a contributory factor in a number of infant sleep-related deaths.

> 'I think people were quite shocked at the life circumstances of these babies because a lot of the poverty and multi-generational stuff people are vaguely aware of it but many of these babies lived in circumstances that the average British Columbian wouldn't imagine.'

In a review of aboriginal deaths in WA a number of infant sleep-related deaths occurred in situations in which large families were living in overcrowded, very deprived circumstances (Frances *et al.*, 2008). In some regions of Australia the presence of poverty, ethnicity and remoteness may constitute multiple risk factors for some families.

> 'You're dealing with impossible circumstances in very remote areas, dealing with incredibly complex difficulties and challenging circumstances ... some of the issues are extremely difficult — just basic housing, clean water, sewerage and a place to put your rubbish collection.'

Some CDR teams in Australia have recruited aboriginal staff to enable them to develop better relationships with aboriginal communities in an attempt to maximise the prevention potential of community programmes in remote areas.

> '... because of resourcing it just hasn't been possible to do as much of it as we'd like but we've got additional resources and a more proactive programme now. We've been able to secure some additional resources, and the approach of a programme focus on outreach has really meant the office as a whole has gone leaps and bounds in terms of our understanding of the area.'

Children known to the child protection system may also be at greater risk of dying. One local CDR group reported that around 30% of all child deaths in their region were known to child welfare agencies at some point in their life. A substantial proportion of unsafe sleeping deaths are of children known to child welfare agencies, and a number of CDR teams have recognised that prevention activity needs to focus on these vulnerable families. While children living in families known to child protection agencies may be at greater risk than children not known to child protection agencies they are not necessarily at greater risk of dying from an abuse- or neglect-related death. Most of the children known to child welfare agencies do not die from abuse or neglect; they die from accidental injury, and they may be at increased risk of accidental injury due to poverty, lack of parental supervision or because they have a higher propensity for risk-taking behaviour.

Prevention of fire deaths, Ontario

A review of fire deaths in Ontario found that children from families known to CPSs were thirty-two times more likely to die in fires and might require considerable education around child safety (Office of the Chief Coroner for Ontario, 2011). The review found that fire play by preschool children was the number one cause of fire death. Other risk factors included smoke alarm functionality and fire escape behaviour.

The review concluded that there was a need to redirect intervention at high-risk families – those known to CPSs and families with preschool children. It recommended that primary care physicians were the most appropriate professionals to educate families routinely during parent/child health examinations, because they had the most trusting relationships with families. They now educate smokers to stop smoking and keep matches and lighters out of the way; enquire into fire setting and fire play behaviour; and if necessary refer children for counselling or psychiatry.

The review also resulted in considerable practice change in the child welfare system. A manual was developed for child welfare workers around checking for fire safety, and they now look at hazards in the home as a matter of course.

CONCLUSION

- The main reasons why children die are remarkably consistent across Australia, New Zealand, the US, Canada and the UK: they die from natural causes; they die unexpectedly in their sleep; they also die from injuries caused by road traffic accidents, drowning, fire or poisoning. Some die from intentional injury through suicide. Only a very small number die as a result of interpersonal violence.
- Unsafe sleeping, substance misuse, lack of parental supervision and risk-taking behaviour of adolescents are key themes across countries. Age, gender, ethnicity, poverty, living in a remote area and being known to child protection agencies may be associated with increased risks for some types of deaths.
- CDR has informed our knowledge of risk factors for different types of deaths and led to the development of national, state and local prevention strategies in Australia, NZ, North America and the UK.
- Prevention initiatives normally comprise a range of strategies including environmental modification, produce modification, legislation and regulation, promotion of the use of safety devices, home visits to families and education.

CHAPTER 6

Demonstrating impact and effectiveness and maximising learning

Introduction

Demonstrating that CDR is having an impact can be difficult.

> **'We do need evidence but quite a lot of what we do is quite intangible.'**
>
> **'One of the challenges with CDR in general is that it works best when it's done locally. We get a pretty good idea of how children die nationally and where the public health prevention efforts are, but the specific circumstances — the ideas that will give us points of leverage to say this is where we could intervene with families to try to prevent this — that only comes out with the level of detail that you can get from a local CDR. But at a local level even in big counties you're not doing that many cases of any particular death over the course of a year, so it's very hard to say that we have a great crib giveaway programme in our county and the numbers of deaths associated with unsafe sleep have gone down. Having said that there are places where they actually make that claim I think. Philadelphia has pretty good data to show that they've impacted that through specific recommendations.'**

This chapter discusses the issues and challenges for CDR teams in relation to monitoring recommendations and demonstrating impact and effectiveness. It also considers how the learning from CDR can be maximised by undertaking thematic reviews and adopting a project approach to feed into improved policy and practice.

MONITORING RECOMMENDATIONS

The quality of the recommendations made by CDR teams has rarely been subjected to evaluation. Many states in the US have had CDR for several decades now, but with the exception of Georgia (Kellermann *et al.*, 1999) CDR teams have never been formally evaluated so we do not know how effective they are (Douglas and Cunningham, 2008). Douglas and Cunningham (2008) reviewed 338 recommendations from CDR teams in thirty-seven US states. They found that the most commonly cited recommendation was an increase in public education, including general parent education, safe sleeping environments, fire safety, motor-vehicle-related neglect and shaken baby syndrome. Increased training for professionals, changes to and improvements in child death investigations and improvements in risk factors and assessment were other often noted recommendations.

One of the strengths of CDR teams is that unlike coroners they can look across multiple cases and follow up on recommendations.

> 'Coroners don't have the power to pursue a recommendation and make sure it's enforced. For example, the coroner made a recommendation about a road following the death of a young girl and land transport NZ politely declined to do anything but we were able to take that to our group and discuss it, we've got the potential for a broader reach.'

Being able to monitor the implementation of recommendations effectively is, however, a significant challenge for CDR teams. As seen in previous chapters many states, provinces and countries have legislative mandates in place requiring CDR teams to report on their findings and/or make recommendations to policymakers, but CDR teams also need to be able to monitor their recommendations over time to find out whether they have been successfully implemented and to demonstrate they are actually making a difference. Updates on implementation of past recommendations need to be reported on at regular intervals. In the US only seven states require a response to their recommendations (Wirtz *et al.*, 2011).

Some CDR teams do not have the resources to take forward or track their recommendations. Some prioritise recommendations or focus on a small number: for example, Colorado has 'top' recommendations. Some teams give their recommendations to others to take forward and implement rather than doing this work themselves. Where this is the case teams need to ensure they get all the key players involved. In some states in the US Safekids coalitions take recommendations forward. In a number of states and provinces in the US and Canada review teams do not have responsibility for implementing recommendations, because there is a separate implementation process distinct from the review process. For example:

- in Wisconsin an advisory committee considers aggregate data and makes recommendations for legislative change;
- in Alaska an advisory board meets quarterly and acts on one recommendation at a time (for example, winter safety);
- in Maryland there is a separate community action team and neighbourhood action team with representatives from families and neighbourhood organisations.

Accountability is an important issue. As Pearson (2008) asked in relation to CDR processes in the UK, who is responsible if recommendations for prevention are made but not carried through — if, for example, children continue to die from preventable road accidents. This question is equally applicable in other countries. Newton *et al.* (2010) have recommended that agencies in Australia should be legally required to act on the recommendations of CDR in order to increase accountability.

South Australia's legislation is useful because it stipulates that the CDR team must monitor the implementation of their recommendations.

> 'Our legislation says we make and monitor recommendations. We make recommendations to the minister and then we monitor their implementation and I think that's for me the area of greatest interest, how you monitor whether you've made a difference. At the moment as with a lot of committees we make our recommendations, we get back the responses from various departments about what they're doing and how they are doing it and then we really just enter into a dialogue about that. Usually they'll say 'yes we're doing that' and it becomes a kind of a dialogue where you eventually come to some understanding or through that process sort of get to a point where you're saying 'well actually how are you implementing that?' and 'how are you going about describing or evaluating whether your practice

> has changed?' And I think that's clearly where most teams are at now — saying how do we best monitor how change has been achieved? And I guess that's the interesting issue in child death review now as teams have grown. I think you can see teams go through a kind of pattern of growth or development where you do your reviews, you make your recommendations and after a few years they come to be very similar and you start to question especially within the child protection systems ... okay you know we've made the recommendations now, we're being told they've got policies and processes in place ... so where to from here? How do you get down to knowing that change has occurred?'

Ontario requires a response to recommendations within a certain time frame, and responses are included in their annual report. Victoria also uses annual reports to track the success of recommendations over time. In BC the implementation of recommendations is similarly tracked and monitored and reported on in annual reports. Its annual reports acknowledge successful prevention initiatives by awarding gold stars to organisations that have demonstrated excellence in promoting and protecting child health and safety.

> 'We give gold stars. We believe in congratulating and acknowledging the work that's underway.'

> The CDRU's stars are a testament to the province's collective commitment to reducing the number of preventable child deaths in British Columbia and beyond (CDRU, 2010).

Vancouver Island Health Authority was awarded a gold star for 'baby's own bed' — an initiative to promote culturally appropriate messaging about safe sleep. BC also acknowledges work that has happened without the need for the CDR team to make a recommendation.:

> '... we had a couple of motor vehicle crashes on a certain part of the highway on the island and the police were involved and the ministry of transportation and highways, and they created a change in the grade. That was done without a recommendation, but it was linked to some child deaths and other deaths.'

One member of the CDR team in BC has specific responsibility for examining the data, considering what is known about best practice and turning review findings into recommendations for action.

DEMONSTRATING EFFECTIVENESS

Even if teams can ensure that recommendations are implemented and reported on it is still very difficult to evaluate outcomes, demonstrate effectiveness and prove that CDR actually makes a difference. There is a growing body of evidence on the effectiveness of CDR, but much of it relates to the process rather than to specific outcomes for children (Bunting and Reid, 2005; Vincent, 2010). While it is difficult to attribute causal linkages there are, however, many examples of information from CDR being used to develop actions to prevent injuries and deaths.

> 'Sometimes we worry we're not making a difference and the numbers aren't going down ... but I think a lot of good has happened.'

EFFECTIVENESS CAN BE MEASURED BY

- monitoring the implementation of recommendations;
- evidence of policy/legislative change;
- evidence of practice change and improvement – identification of practice gaps, improved staff knowledge/education;
- measuring the extent to which parents' and young people's behaviour has been modified;
- determining the extent to which deaths have been prevented.

One of the best measures of effectiveness is obviously the extent to which CDR succeeds in reducing the number of child deaths, and one of the reasons why some people are sceptical about the effectiveness of CDR is because it is difficult to demonstrate that it actually saves lives. There is some evidence that some types of deaths have been prevented as a result of CDR activity. Despite an increase in pool numbers, for example, there has been a continuing decline in numbers of drowning deaths since pool fencing legislation was introduced in New Zealand: twenty-two children died a year from drowning prior to legislation, whereas three children die a year now.

> These improvements highlight the benefits of using a mechanical barrier in addition to the expectation of constant supervision (double protection) to prevent drowning in infants and young children (CYMRC, 2010).

Although individuals involved in CDR acknowledge that this cannot be wholly attributed to recommendations from CDR, evidence from CDR certainly played a key role in identifying the need for legislation. One individual reported that when a politician suggested that legislation might be unnecessary the national review committee was able to supply numbers from CDR as evidence to support maintaining the legislation.

Further examples were provided in other countries.

> 'There was a period where a number of children were being run over in driveways. There was a lot of work that we did with the the road transports authority and the motor accidents authority, which really resulted in looking at the design of cars, and having information in the public arena about the dangers, pamphlets that spoke about fencing driveways. And there was a reduction in those deaths. Those deaths went down to zero for a few years. They've gone up again, but I think that's an example. I think that the changes that there have been to licensing in NSW for drivers — young drivers — can be traced back to the work of the CDR team or the monitoring of these deaths for these children. Driver fatalities have decreased. You know I'm not saying this is all causal but I think the CDR team is there in the mix of the relationship into all this. Sleeping deaths — I think the CDR team has been going on about this for quite a while and I think it's made an impact. Again it's not causal. What it does is it forces agencies to do things and through the agencies doing things then practice changes. I can imagine that today the Minister for Health would have sent out an internal email saying to every maternity hospital: 'you make sure in your hospital today to make sure that infants are not left in bed with their parents' so the change might just be immediate, it might just be for a short-term

period; it might be medium; it might be long term, but there is change and if you keep going on about it then the change continues. In relation to take-home methadone there was a change made in relation to the cap that was put on methadone. I know this is ridiculous but they weren't child safe caps before — they are now.'

Child abuse and neglect (CAN) homicides and unsafe sleeping deaths in Sacramento, California

Birth and Beyond – an $8 million comprehensive home visitation programme came out of Sacramento, California CDR team recommendations in 1999. Wirtz *et al.* (2011) have documented how the CDR team worked with local leaders to assess the current resources and political context and recommended the formation of a high-level task force to create and sustain evidence-based home visitation services. Birth and Beyond targeted eight high-risk neighbourhoods. Following the programme's implementation, the CDR team documented a significant decline in child maltreatment homicides. They undertook a five-year statistical analysis looking at a rolling five-year average of rates and detected a statistically significant decline from 1997–2001 to 2003–7. When 'Birth and beyond' was created in 1997 there were fourteen CAN homicides compared to one in 2003 (the year that Birth and Beyond and other programmes such as Black Infant Health and Nurse Family Partnership were all fully funded).

> 'When you've got fully funded programmes that are out there educating parents and decreasing stressors in parents' lives there are going to be less CAN homicides.'

The number of CAN homicides has recently increased again in Sacramento: in 2011 there were twelve CAN homicides compared to three in the previous year.

> 'When we did last year's report we noticed there had been an increase in CAN homicides. There isn't yet a long enough time period to see if it's significant, but numbers are going up and it was at this time — 2009–10 — that Birth and Beyond lost its funding altogether. Luckily we've now got alternative funding to continue it.'

The CDR team produced a graph of funding levels over the years compared to the number of CAN homicides and found that:

> '... at the point where there was the most funding for Birth and Beyond there were the least CAN homicides'.

Safe sleeping was another example cited in Sacramento. Sacramento used to have 24–27 unsafe sleeping deaths a year using an umbrella classification of SIDs, SUIDs (SIDS with risk factors such as co-sleeping or bed sharing) and undetermined deaths. Following implementation of a safe sleeping campaign – The Safe Beginnings Collaborative – the numbers of unsafe sleeping deaths halved.

> **'The funding went away and numbers have gone right back up. It's not a scientific study, but you can't just have a campaign and then leave an issue as new parents are born every day, so two years ago we applied for funding again and said 'numbers are going up and we need to develop a much stronger prevention campaign and target education to new parents at risk.'**

Ultimately we would hope that evidence-based prevention initiatives that come out of CDR will result in a reduction in the number of deaths. Unfortunately most CDR teams are struggling to demonstrate that their prevention initiatives are having an impact on numbers of child deaths. It may be difficult to demonstrate that CDR actually prevents children dying, but it certainly has a role to play in protecting children, and CDR findings have influenced policy and practice changes at local, state and national level. Despite the challenges, as described in the previous chapter, there have been successful prevention programmes initiated in response to the findings of CDR in Australia, NZ, North America and the UK.

CDR teams can and sometimes do undertake process evaluations: for example, if they want to measure the effectiveness of safe sleeping initiatives that have resulted from CDR recommendations they might try to find out whether babies who leave hospital have a safe sleeping environment at home. It is possible to evaluate these types of things, but assessing real impact and outcomes is far more difficult.

One of the aims of a co-sleeping cohort study that was undertaken in NSW, and is discussed later in this chapter, was to reduce the numbers of deaths where co-sleeping and parental substance misuse coexisted. While the overall numbers of deaths where co-sleeping is a feature have fallen in NSW in recent years — and the co-sleeping campaign has undoubtedly played a part in this — the numbers of deaths known to the DOCS, where there is also evidence of parental substance misuse, have not fallen. This does not mean that the co-sleeping project has failed. The project was also designed to result in practice improvement and change. One of the ways in which it aimed to do this was by improving staff knowledge and education, and there is evidence to suggest that it has achieved this. Staff reported that they are now more confident in approaching the issues with parents. Although there have been further cases where children have died documentary evidence and interviews with staff confirmed that workers are discussing the risks with parents, providing them with advice and where appropriate with resources to purchase cots and bedding. What is most difficult to change is not professional practice but parental behaviour. Staff may now routinely outline the risks to parents, but this does not guarantee that parents will not share a sleeping surface with their babies. There is unlikely to be a significant impact on the numbers of deaths of children at highest risk unless parents' behaviour can be modified, but CDR teams in Australia, NZ, North America and the UK are struggling to modify parents' behaviour.

> 'We've been pretty successful in turning round the minds of the child welfare system in Ontario and public health and some of the medical people ... so we think in terms of professionals we've made some gains. The difficulty is the numbers aren't down in terms of deaths ... How do we determine if the professionals are giving the messages and they're still not abiding by them ... it's an emotional issue ... 70% of people sleep with kids and their argument is we get a better sleep with that kid, we take precautions, we think it through, we know the risks ... so we've done a little work on trying to figure out which are the high-risk kids ... I think it's too ubiquitous in the culture, everybody does it.'

> 'In relation to safe sleeping messages I think people have got a bit complacent and they need to be reminded — people need to be constantly reminded about behaviour.'

CDR teams appear to be struggling particularly in relation to safe sleeping messaging, because findings are inconclusive. While CDR data has demonstrated a link between unsafe sleeping and infant deaths it is not possible to say that all children who died in unsafe sleeping environments would have lived if they had been sleeping in a safe environment.

> 'Messaging is so tough in this area ... should we be going for risk elimination or risk reduction? And the safest place for

> a kid to be, I have no problem recognising this and totally supporting this, is in a crib and on their back ... The middle upper class don't have as many deaths as we do in the population of child protection. They have smaller beds, they have less modern stuff, they have more drugs and alcohol, more cramped quarters ... so how do you measure all that? I think it's very complex. The other challenge is are all these kids dying from their unsafe environment? Clearly there are some where we can absolutely say they're sleeping on a couch. There's not really any question in my mind with those ones, but we still classify them as undetermined. Then you've got them in this unsafe sleep environment in an adult bed with a comforter that's nearby and they're dead, and although we can't find a metabolic thing or a cardiac thing we know that's possible, so there's different rankings of unsafe sleep ... what's really unsafe and what's safe and so on ...If we could concretely say these are all deaths from this sleep environment we'd be able to give a stronger message but do I know they are? I don't.'

Value for money

A question that is sometimes asked of CDR is whether it represents good value for money and whether, for example, resources might be better spent on providing direct services to children and young people. Some individuals involved in CDR acknowledge that CDR teams need to do a better job of being able to demonstrate value for money.

In New Zealand CDR costs NZ$1.5 million a year. It is a relatively expensive process, because central funding is provided to local groups. As an individual involved in CDR pointed out, however, this sum is tiny when compared to the enormous financial costs of injury — to the NZ$400 million spent on Accident Compensation Corporation (ACC) payments to young people with complex injuries in New Zealand every year; or to the cost of care for a single shaken baby that can amount to NZ$20 million over a lifetime. If we consider these kinds of comparisons even if CDR succeeds in preventing only one death a year it may represent good value for money.

'I personally think if I can save one life it's worth it.'

'You can't put a price on saving a child's life.'

LEARNING THROUGH THEMATIC ANALYSIS/PROJECT APPROACHES

'Bridging that gap from a whole load of files to changes in social policy and legislation and change on the ground that's when in our mind the review is finished.'

For CDR to have a prevention focus it needs to be able to identify trends at state or national as well as local level, and prevention programmes to target these trends need to be developed at both local and national level. An evidence-based approach to practice improvement through a model of individual review, cross-case review and cohort review, which exists in some states, provinces and countries, can result in real learning and practice change.

LEARNING MODEL

- Individual reviews to examine practice in relation to an individual case
- Cross-case analysis — generates a body of evidence over time to enable identification of trends and themes
- Cohort/group analyses/reviews to improve learning about particular types of deaths or issues
- Project approach to ensure learning leads to improved practice and policy
- Positive outcomes for children including reduced numbers of deaths

'We're interested in preventable deaths and quite reasonably we don't want to direct resources to or put the department through an investigation unless it's really going to be for some kind of learning that's going to prevent deaths in the future. So that's our focus — it's about preventable deaths and what can we learn from the death of a child that's just occurred? On a case-by-case basis we can obviously bring about change and can make recommendations with the

> departments. But we can also look at cases on a group basis — you know, if there are systemic issues that are coming through in individual cases we can adopt a project kind of approach.'

Collating the data from individual reviews at a state or national level and undertaking regular analyses of this data enable a large database of information to be built up. Once data has been collected for a number of years it can be used to identify particular trends or issues that may require further investigation and analysis. In New Zealand the national review group reported that they have been able to do this only after seven years of data collection. They now have enough data to be able to drill into different types of deaths, and to look at specific issues in more detail using cross-case analysis. They have looked, for example, in detail at SUDI deaths, at drownings of children under the age of five, at unintentional injury in young people, and at suicide, and they have reported on all these issues in their annual report. The NZ national review group was unable to do this in its first few years of operation because it was conscious of the dangers of working with too small numbers. The national system in Wales also encountered difficulties in its first few years of operation because it was working with such small numbers.

Discussion of individual cases is necessary in terms of accountability and useful in terms of making recommendations to effect local change, but in order to make a real impact on prevention CDR also needs to look beyond individual cases. Annual trends in rates and risk factors can be identified in annual reports, and recommendations can then be made, which look across all circumstances of death. This can lead to identification of specific issues or circumstances that require more in-depth analysis and targeted action. A number of Australian states and Canadian provinces annually review all their data and use the findings from this analysis to identify particular issues or themes that they want to investigate further through a themed cohort or group analysis, which looks across a cluster of cases.

> Analysis of common themes and systemic issues arising from a group of similar deaths can be a worthwhile exercise. Its value is undoubtedly enhanced by the direct and

> collaborative involvement of those charged with responsibility for system reform (VCDRC, 1999, p. 82).

> The group analysis process allows for more comprehensive examination of the issues arising from a particular group of deaths, within the context of current research and practice knowledge. It provides for the identification of best practice principles, as well as current gaps or deficits in service provision (VCDRC, 2008 p. 7).

Cumulative harm, Victoria

The CDR committee in Victoria undertakes a rigorous qualitative analysis of all cases they review over a year, and their annual reports focus on new themes that have emerged from looking across all cases. It may then recommend that a group analysis be undertaken on a new theme or issue that has been identified. In 2005/6 its annual report identified chronic neglect and cumulative harm as key factors in many of the deaths it reviewed that year (VCDRC, 2006). Neglect manifested itself in terms of parents' failure to provide food, clothing, shelter, education, supervision, emotional support and maternal care, all of which are needed in order to achieve healthy development. Cumulative harm referred to patterns of circumstances and events in a child's life that reduced their sense of safety, stability and well-being, such as multiple episodes of abuse or layers of neglect. Practitioners tended to focus on episodic assessment and immediate safety and did not always appreciate the impact of cumulative harm.

Concerns around policy and practice in relation to neglect were identified through CDR. The CDR committee was concerned that some of the children whose deaths it had reviewed had failed to meet the threshold for concern, which was required for intervention by the child protection system. It was also worried that many of the children had been the subject of multiple notifications, and prior notifications can be indicators of a cumulative pattern of harm. It recommended that a group analysis of chronic neglect be undertaken and that the key findings of this analysis be reported on in the following year's annual report. The group analysis was designed to examine the effectiveness of responses by child protection and related services to chronic neglect and to contribute to discussion surrounding chronic neglect and cumulative harm. It was intended that the learning arising from a small group of child deaths would be used to shape future policy and practice.

The group analysis involved examination of the deaths of ten children from 2004–6. Neglect was not a cause of death but was a major risk factor in the lives of these ten children. The analysis used a grounded theory approach. An extensive literature review was also conducted and the findings were presented thematically within an ecological framework.

The analysis considered the way that mental health, domestic violence and substance misuse impacted on parenting.

The findings from the group analysis were used to develop effective responses to chronic neglect. The report highlighted the need for a cumulative harm perspective to be incorporated into all risk assessments. Other findings were that neglect could occur in the context of children having complex medical needs or disabilities that increased the level of parenting required and the vulnerability of the child to lack of appropriate care. Most of the children were also found to live in rural settings. The report concluded that intervention should focus on a whole of community approach (VCDRC, 2006). Health promotion was identified as one strand to support the health and welfare of the child and educate the community on the potential risks to the child. The CDR committee used the findings of the group analysis to make seventeen recommendations.

The learning from the group analysis was used to inform policy and practice directly. The project was undertaken during a time of legislative and policy reform within Victoria's child protection and family support system and was timely in terms of being able to influence this reform. The impact of cumulative harm was recognised in a new policy and legislative framework in Victoria as a result of this project. The Children, Youth and Families Act 2005 and accompanying practice guidance and tools for staff gave greater attention to the cumulative effects of neglect and abuse on children's longer-term well-being and development and represented a shift away from an episodic focus on immediate harm to enable a more holistic assessment of the child's lived experience.

The CDR committee has followed up and continues to follow up on the outcomes of the neglect group analysis. The DHS provides twice annual feedback to the CDR committee concerning actions taken in relation to recommendations. The annual report that followed the group analysis indicated that the majority of the seventeen recommendations made by the CDR committee had been implemented by human services. Victoria's annual reports also highlight elements of positive case practice, and it is interesting that the annual report that was published a year after the group analysis on chronic neglect included recognition of the impact of cumulative trauma as an example of positive practice.

Group analyses or cohort projects are not just research exercises; they are often undertaken in collaboration with professionals and their aim is to facilitate practice learning. This approach to learning has a robust evidence base because the findings from a large group of cases are used to inform practice and policy rather than the findings from a single case.

> 'On a case-by-case basis we can obviously bring about change and can make recommendations with the departments. But

we can also look at cases on a group basis. You know if there are systemic issues that are coming through in individual cases we can adopt a project kind of approach.'

Themed cohort reviews have been undertaken on a number of issues in Australia, Canada and Wales including:

- deaths from methadone ingestion;
- deaths from neglect;
- deaths from physical abuse;
- deaths related to co-sleeping;
- deaths from suicide;
- drowning deaths;
- fire deaths;
- deaths of aboriginal children;
- deaths of aboriginal children where chronic neglect was a factor;
- deaths where domestic violence was a factor.

In both NSW and WA annual review of state data revealed that aboriginal children were significantly over-represented in CDRs. Both of these states, therefore, decided to undertake cohort reviews of cases involving aboriginal children. NSW undertook a group analysis on all deaths of aboriginal children. WA reviewed all the deaths of aboriginal children where neglect was a factor, not necessarily in the child's death, but where neglect had featured in the history of the case (Frances *et al.*, 2008). The aim of both these cohort studies was to identify how practice could be improved to meet the needs of aboriginal families better. In NSW a subcommittee comprising aboriginal practitioners, aboriginal services branch, learning and development, and an aboriginal reference group developed an aboriginal child deaths practice solutions seminar using an action learning model to deliver learning from review to all frontline staff. A DVD was made which stressed the importance of addressing safety alongside cultural considerations. Eighty-eight sessions were undertaken in forty localities involving 1,100 staff.

Safe sleeping project, New South Wales

New South Wales uses a project approach to ensure evidence from CDR promotes learning and brings about practice improvement. A project approach was adopted to tackle the issue of babies who died in unsafe sleeping environments. Analysis of data from CDR identified that a high and increasing number of healthy babies had died accidentally after sharing a sleeping surface with one or both parents. In a high proportion of these cases the review team also found that there was evidence of parental substance misuse. Although these families were known to the DOCS in none of these cases was there any suggestion that parents deliberately intended to harm their child. The deaths were all accidental but potentially preventable. The overwhelming message that could be taken from this evidence from CDR was that parents should not sleep with their babies when they had used alcohol or drugs.

The main aim of the co-sleeping cohort project was to understand the practice implications of this evidence and to improve practice in this area. The specific practice aims were to increase staff awareness of the dangers of co-sleeping when parents used substances and to increase their confidence and skills so they would be able to tackle the issue positively with parents and provide them with clear advice about the risks. Ultimately it was hoped that practice improvement in this area would result in a reduction in the numbers of child deaths where co-sleeping and substance misuse coexisted.

The project team visited two areas of high drug dependency to explore some of the issues. It also ran an inter-agency session to explore what the policy and practice direction around co-sleeping was in health and community services and found that staff were given very little direction. It used a method of learning it had practised successfully in previous cohort projects: it held a seminar that was divided into two separate sessions. The first session included a presentation to staff of the findings from child death reviews around co-sleeping and parental substance misuse as well as findings from wider research on this issue. It also included the presentation of a case study to facilitate reflective learning, which included role-playing of the interaction with clients. The second session was what members of the project team referred to as the 'Asking the hard questions' session. In small groups staff talked about the barriers to discussing the risks with parents. They were asked to come up with solutions to tackling these barriers and to present these back to the larger group. One of the members of the project team reported that the aim of this session was to get the message across to staff that 'leaving the practice of co-sleeping unchallenged could be as dangerous as leaving a child with a black eye'.

The main finding in relation to practice barriers was that staff were not confident about challenging parents. They were reluctant to intervene for a variety of reasons: some felt they were not in a position to comment because they had co-slept with their own children; some believed that co-sleeping was positive because it promoted attachment or breastfeeding and cited research evidence around this; others felt that they could not raise the issue with aboriginal families because co-sleeping was a cultural practice. The cohort study concluded that there was a need to ensure that staff had accurate information about the risks and had the skills and confidence to transmit this information to parents in a non-patronising way, but in a way that would get the message across – the message being that children can and have died because they have shared beds with parents. The project team developed a number of resources: fact sheets were designed for staff outlining the findings from CDR and providing clear information about the risks; other resources – posters, brochures, wallet size information and fridge magnets – were designed for staff to use to raise the issues with parents. The parental resources provided clear advice about the dangers of co-sleeping, outlining safe and unsafe practice and can easily be understood by people with low levels of literacy; aboriginal specific resources were also developed.

In terms of reasons why parents shared sleeping surfaces with their babies, the cohort study found that poverty, overcrowding and transience were major factors, particularly among the aboriginal population. Discussions with aboriginal advisers and parents confirmed that co-sleeping was not in fact a cultural practice. It was, however, a fairly prevalent practice because many families did not have access to cots or safe bedding. Large families were also a risk factor. Some families had several children close together in age and only one cot. In order to tackle these issues resources were made available so that staff could provide families with money to purchase portable and non-portable cots and safe bedding. Staff were told to ask to view sleeping arrangements on home visits and to offer advice on how to make up a cot safely.

Another reason why parents said they shared sleeping surfaces with their babies was because they found it difficult to settle them. A significant proportion of the babies who had died had been born with neonatal abstinence syndrome, which would have made them particularly hard to settle. The parental resources that were developed therefore included phone numbers that parents could ring to obtain advice on settling techniques. Staff were also able to refer parents to family support services, which could provide help with settling.

The cohort study also found that in a high proportion of cases where children died parents were not hard drug users; neither were they consuming vast quantities of alcohol. Many of them used only cannabis or took prescribed painkillers or tranquillisers. This was an important message because staff often minimalised the risks from cannabis use and prescribed drugs in comparison with those from harder drugs. A lot of work was, therefore, done to ensure that this message was conveyed to staff and taken into account when assessing risk.

Suicide is another theme that has been identified through annual review of child death data as warranting further attention in several states. Annual review has demonstrated an increase in suicide deaths in a number of Australian states, particularly in the numbers of aboriginal suicide deaths. Some states have, therefore, reviewed all suicide deaths to identify how they can improve the service response for young people at risk of suicide. Wales, BC and Ontario have also undertaken reviews of suicide deaths to inform prevention activity.

Cohort reviews have also been undertaken where smaller numbers of deaths have been identified: for example, in NSW a cohort study of deaths from methadone ingestion was undertaken because annual findings from CDR identified a small but increasing number of cases in which children had died after ingesting their parents' methadone. Monitoring of data from CDR can, therefore, enable identification of small but nevertheless important trends in types of cases.

Themed analyses do not necessarily have to focus on different types of death. In New Zealand the national committee is starting to look at the themes of under-supervision, interpersonal violence and alcohol and drugs in addition to suicide, SUDI and other themes, because it believes these are constant themes irrespective of how a child actually dies. In all cases it is possible to consider whether under-supervision or alcohol and drugs were factors in the death. An individual involved in CDR acknowledged that CDR teams have been very successful in terms of looking at vertical streams but less successful in sorting data by these types of horizontal streams.

CONCLUSION

Being able to monitor the implementation of recommendations can be a significant challenge for CDR teams. Even if their legislation enables them to do this it may still be difficult to demonstrate that CDR recommendations are having an impact in terms of improving outcomes for children. CDR has undoubtedly resulted in changes to legislation and policy and significant practice change, but it is extremely difficult to demonstrate that it has impacted on the overall number of child deaths. A significant proportion of deaths are closely related to parents' behaviour or young people's risk-taking behaviour, and modifying these factors can be particularly challenging. It is unlikely that CDR will ever succeed in preventing all deaths from non-natural causes.

> **'The team talks about wouldn't it be great to get to the point where you never have to have a CDR team but that to my mind will never be the case because of the nature of human behaviour. People will forget if they're not continually reminded that what they are doing is stupid and they will keep doing it.'**

While CDR teams may not be able to prevent all child deaths this book has demonstrated that they have a major role to play in informing prevention initiatives and can and have reduced the numbers of some types of deaths. CDR is a comprehensive, evidence-based approach to understanding and preventing child mortality that:

- helps us understand how and why children die so we can prevent future deaths and improve child safety;
- is a key source of accurate information on and has improved our understanding of shaken baby syndrome, youth suicide, infant deaths associated with bed sharing, substance use and other risk factors;
- has led to prevention campaigns to tackle safe sleeping, suicide and other deaths;
- has contributed to knowledge about abuse and neglect and led to policies and initiatives that have made major contributions to keeping children safe;
- has been used to identify special population groups that need to be targeted and/or culturally responsive prevention programmes.

In the words of an individual involved in CDR.

> **'I talk about honouring the child that's died because that's what we are doing. You can't make it right for them but it's about taking the learning to the living.'**

REFERENCES

Axford, N. and Bullock, R. (2005) *Child Death and Significant Case Reviews: International Approaches*, Edinburgh: Scottish Executive

Brandon, M., Belderson, P., Warren, C., Howe, D., Gardner, R., Dodsworth, J. and Black, J. (2008) *Analysing Child Deaths and Serious Injury Through Abuse and Neglect: What Can We Learn?*, London: Department for Children, Schools and Families

Brandon, M., Bailey, S. and Belderson, P. (2009) *Understanding Serious Case Reviews and Their Impact: A Biennial Analysis of Serious Case Reviews*, London: Department for Children, Schools and Families

Brandon, M., Howe, D., Black, J. and Dodsworth, J. (2002) *Learning How to Make Children Safer Part 2: An Analysis for the Welsh Office of Serious Child Abuse Cases in Wales*, Cardiff: University of East Anglia/Welsh Office

Bunting, L. and Reid, C. (2005) 'Reviewing child deaths: Learning from the American experience', *Child Abuse Review*, Vol. 14, No. 2, pp. 82–96

CDRU (2009) *Safe and Sound: A Five Year Retrospective*, Vancouver: British Columbia Coroners Service

CDRU (2010) *Annual Report*, Vancouver: British Columbia Coroners Service

CDSIRC (2010) *Annual Report 2009–2010*, Adelaide: Government of South Australian Institute of Family Studies

Children's Health Alliance of Wisconsin (n.d.) *Keeping Kids Alive in Wisconsin Child Death Review team Guidelines*, Milwaukee, WI: Children's Health Alliance of Wisconsin

Christian, C. W. and Sege, R .D. (2010) 'Policy statement — child fatality review', *Pediatrics*, Vol. 126, No. 3, pp. 592–6

Corby, B. (2003) 'Towards a new means of inquiry into child abuse cases', *Journal of Social Welfare and Family Law*, Vol. 25, No. 3, pp. 229–41

Corby, B., Doig, A. and Roberts, V. (2001) *Public Inquiries into Abuse of Children in Residential Care*, London: Jessica Kingsley

Covington, T. (2011) 'The US national child death review case reporting system', *Injury Prevention*, Vol. 17, No. 1, pp. 134–7

Covington, T. and Wirtz, S. (forthcoming) 'The Power of Child Death Review to Prevent Maltreatment' in Alexander, S; Alexander, R. and Guterman, N. *Prevention of Child Maltreatment*, GW Medical

CSSIW (2009) *Improving Practice to Protect Children in Wales: An Examination of the Role of Serious Case Reviews*, Cardiff: Care and Social Services Inspectorate Wales

CYMRC (2009) *Fifth Report to the Minister of Health Reporting Mortality 2002–2008*. Wellington: Child and Youth Mortality Review Committee

DCSF (2009) *Preventable Child Deaths in England: Year Ending 31 March 2009*,

London: Department for Children Schools and Families

Department for Education (2010) *Preventable Child Deaths in England: Year Ending 31 March 2010*. London: Department for Education

Department of Health, Home Office, Department for Education and Employment (1999) *Working Together To Safeguard Children*, London: The Stationery Office

Desapriya, E., Sones, M., Ramanzin, T. *et al.* (2011) 'Injury prevention in child death review: child pedestrian fatalities', *Injury Prevention*, Vol. 17, No. 1, pp. i4–i9

Douglas, E. M. and Cunningham, J. M. (2008) 'Recommendations from child fatality review teams: results of a US nationwide exploratory study concerning maltreatment fatalities and social service delivery', *Child Abuse Review*, Vol. 17, pp. 331–51

Durfee, M., Durfee, D. T. and West, M. P. (2002) 'Child fatality review: an international movement', *Child Abuse and Neglect*, Vol. 26, Nos 6–7, pp. 619–36

Falkov, A. (1996) *A Study of Working Together Part 8 Reports: Fatal Child Abuse and Parental Psychiatric Disorder*, London: Department of Health

Fleming, P, Tsgot, B. and Blair, P. (2006) 'Modifiable risk factors, sleep environment, developmental physiology and common polymorphisms: understanding and preventing sudden infant deaths', *Early Human Development*, Vol. 82, pp. 761–6

Frances, K., Hutchins, T., Saggers, S. *et al.* (2008) *A Report Prepared for the Western Australian Child Death Review Committee. Group Analysis of Aboriginal Child Death Review Cases in Which Chronic Neglect is Present*, Perth, WA: National Drug Research Institute, Curtin University of Technology

Gibbs, J. (2009) 'Child death inquiry: moving from rhetoric to learning', *Children Australia*, Vol. 34, No. 3, pp. 9–17

HM Government (1989) *Working Together Under the Children Act*, London: The Stationery Office

HM Government (2006) *Working Together to Safeguard Children: A Guide to Interagency Working to Safeguard and Promote the Welfare of Children*, London: The Stationery Office

HM Government (2008) *PSA Delivery Agreement 13: Improve Children and Young People's Safety*, London: The Stationery Office

HM Government (2010) *Working Together to Safeguard Children: A Guide to Interagency Working to Safeguard and Promote the Welfare of Children*, London: The Stationery Office

Hochstadt, N. J. (2006) 'Child death review teams: a vital component of child protection', *Child Welfare*, Vol. 85, No. 4, pp. 633–70

Home Office, Department of Health, Department of Education and Science and Welsh Office (1991) *Working Together Under The Children Act 1989: A Guide to Arrangements for Inter-Agency Co-operation for the Protection of Children from Abuse*, London: Her Majesty's Stationery Office

Hughes, E. N. (2006). *BC Children and Youth Review: An Independent Review of BC's Child Protection System*, Victoria, BC: Ministry for Children and Family Development

Johnston, B. D. and Covington, T. M. (2011) 'Injury prevention in child death review', *Injury Prevention*, Vol. 17, No. 1, pp. i1–i3

Kellermann, A. L. Thomas, W., Henry, G. *et al.* (1999). *The Best of Intentions: An Evaluation of the Child Fatality Review Process in Georgia 2001*, Atlanta, GA: Center for Injury Control, Rollins School of Public Health, Emory University

Laming, Lord (2009) *The Protection of Children in England: A Progress Report.* London: The Stationery Office

Lamont, A. (2010) *Child Deaths from Abuse and Neglect in Australia. National Child Protection Clearing House Resource Sheet*, Melbourne: Australian Institute of Family Studies

Layton, R. A. (2003) *Our Best Investment: A State Plan to Protect and Ensure the Interests of Children*, Adelaide: Children, Youth and Women's Health Service

McDonald, G., Taylor, B., Carter, M. *et al.* (2005) *Circumstances Surrounding Drowning in Those Under 25 Years in New Zealand (1980–2002)*, Wellington: NZ Child and Youth Mortality Review Committee

Morris, L., Williams, L. and Beak, K. (2007) *A Study of Case Reviews Submitted to the Welsh Assembly Government under Chapter 8 of 'Working Together to Safeguard Children: A Guide to Interagency Working to Safeguard and Promote the Welfare of Children'*, Cardiff: University of Wales, Newport/National Assembly for Wales

Munro, E. (2011) *The Munro Review of Child Protection: Final Report A Child Centred System*, London: Department for Education.

NCCDR (2011) *The Status of Child Death Review in the United States in 2010*, Okemos, MI: National Centre for Child Death Review

Newton, R., Frederick, J., Wilson, E. *et al.* (2010) 'Legislation and child death review processes in Australia: understanding our failure to prevent child death', *UNSW Law Journal*, Vol. 33, No. 3, pp. 987–1012

Office of the Chief Coroner for Ontario (2011) *Drowning Review: A Review of All Accidental Drowning Deaths in Ontario from May 1 to September 30 2010*, Toronto: Office of the Chief Coroner

Ofsted (2008) *Learning Lessons, Taking Action: Ofsted's Evaluation of Serious Case Reviews 1 April 2007 to 31 March 2008*, London: Office for Standards in Education, Children's Services and Skills

Ofsted (2009) *Learning Lessons From Serious Case Reviews: Year 2*, London: Office for Standards in Education, Children's Services and Skills

Owen, H. (2009) 'Doing serious case reviews well: politics, academia, risk management and staff care', in Hughes, L. and Owen, H. (2009) *Good Practice in Safeguarding Children*, London: Jessica Kingsley

Owers, M., Brandon, M. and Black, J. (1999) *Learning How to Make Children Safer: An Analysis of Serious Child Abuse Cases in Wales*, Cardiff: University of East Anglia/Welsh Office

Pearson, G. A. (ed.) (2008) *Why Children Die: A Pilot Study 2006, England (South West, North East and West Midlands), Wales and Northern Ireland*, London, Confidential Enquiry into Maternal and Child Health

Quan, L., Pilkey, D., Gomez, A. *et al.* (2011) *Analysis of Pediatric Drowning Deaths in Washington State Using the Child Death Review (CDR) For Surveillance. What CDR Does and Does Not Tell Us About Lethal Drowning Injury*, Seattle: University of Medicine

RCPATH/RCPCH (2004) *Sudden Unexpected Death in Infancy: A Multi-Agency Protocol for Care and Investigation*, London: Royal College of Pathologists/ Royal College of Paediatrics and Child Health

Reder, P. and Duncan, S. (1999) *Lost Innocents: A Follow up Study of Fatal Child Abuse*, London: Routledge

Reder, P., Duncan, S. and Gray, M. (1993) *Child Abuse Tragedies Revisited*, Hove: Brunner-Routledge

Rognum, T. and Willinger, M. (1995) 'The story of the "Stavanger Definition" ', in Tognum, T. (ed.) *Sudden Infant Death Syndrome: New Trends in the Nineties*, Oslo: Scandinavian University Press

Rose, W. and Barnes, J. (2008) *Improving Safeguarding Practice: Study of Serious Case Reviews 2001–2003*. London: Department for Children, Schools and Families

Rose, W. (2010) *Improving Practice to Protect Children in Wales: Developing a New National Framework for Learning and Reviewing*, Cardiff: Welsh Assembly Government

Schnitzer, P. and Ewigman, B. (2005) 'Child deaths resulting from inflicted injuries: household risk factors and perpetrator characteristics'. *Pediatrics*, Vol. 116, pp. 687–93

Selket, K., Palmer, S. and Glover, M. (2010) 'Normalising post-mortems — whose cultural imperative?' Unpublished paper

Sidebotham, P., Brandon, M. and Powell, C. *et al.* (2010) *Learning from Serious Case Reviews: Report of a Research Study on the Methods of Learning Lessons Nationally From Serious Case Reviews*, London: Department for Education

Sidebotham, P., Fox, J., Horwath, J., Powell, C. and Perwez, S. (2008) *Preventing Childhood Deaths: An Observational Study of Child Death Overview Panels in England*, London: Department for Children, Schools and Families

Sinclair, R. and Bullock, R. (2002) *Learning From Past Experience: A Review of Serious Case Reviews*, London: Department of Health

Stafford, A., Parton, N., Vincent, S. *et al.* (2011) *Child Protection Systems in the United Kingdom*, London: Jessica Kingsley

Stone, D. H. (2011) *Injury Prevention in Children*, Edinburgh: Dunedin

US Department of Health and Human Services (2010) *Healthy People 2020*, Washington, DC: US Department of Health and Human Services

VCDRC (1999) *Annual Report of Inquiries into Child Deaths: Protection and Care*, Melbourne: Victorian Child Death Review Committee

VCDRC (2006) *Child Death Group Analysis: Effective Responses to Chronic Neglect*, Melbourne: Office of the Child Safety Commissioner

VCDRC (2008) *Annual Report of Inquiries into Deaths of Children Known to Child Protection 2008*, Melbourne: Victorian Child Death Review Committee

Vincent, S. (2010) *Learning from Child Deaths and Serious Abuse*, Edinburgh: Dunedin

Ward Platt, M. P. (2007) 'Child death reviews: progress in the north of England', *Exchange*, Vol. 4 (Summer)

Webster, R., Schnitzer, P., Jenny, C. *et al.* (2003) 'Child death review: the state of the nation', *American Journal of Preventative Medicine*, Vol. 25, pp. 58–64

Welsh Assembly Government (2006) *Safeguarding Children: Working Together*

under the Children Act 2004, Cardiff: Welsh Assembly Government
Welsh Government (2011) *Protecting Children in Wales: Arrangements for Multi-Agency Child Practice Reviews: Draft Guidance*, Cardiff: Welsh Government
Welsh Government (2012) *Evaluation of the Child Death Review Pilot Project in Wales*, Cardiff: Welsh Government
Wirtz, S. J., Foster, V. and Lenart, G. A. (2011) 'Assessing and improving child death review team recommendations', *Injury Supplement*, Vol. 17, No. 1, p. 1
Wood, J. (2008) *Report of the Special Commission of Inquiry into Child Protection Services in NSW*, Sydney, NSW: NSW Department of Premier and Cabinet
Wood, L. and Naughton, A. (2010) *Procedural Response to Unexpected Deaths in Childhood (PRUDiC)*, Cardiff: Public Health Wales

INDEX

Note: page numbers in italics denote tables